# KEEP VOTING, AMERICA

## STEPHNIE CLARK

iUniverse

An Introduction to

# the United States Family Liberty Plan

as Seen through the Eyes of a

Furious American

Voting Woman

Totally

Fed Up with

Big Brother

# Government!

# KEEP VOTING, AMERICA

iUniverse books may be ordered through booksellers or by contacting:

iUniverse
1663 Liberty Drive
Bloomington, IN 47403
www.iuniverse.com
1-800-Authors (1-800-288-4677)

ISBN: 978-1-5320-3694-1 (sc)
ISBN: 978-1-5320-3695-8 (e)

Library of Congress Control Number: 2017917189

Print information available on the last page.

iUniverse rev. date: 12/12/2017

Liberty is the right to participate in self-government.
So why aren't *you* governing the United States?
Your patriotic side is petitioning you to
*get involved!*

# CONTENTS

UNIT FOUR Appendices

# FOREWORD

**I'm not an educator.**
I'm not a comedy writer.
I don't have many answers.
What I have is a fistful of questions screaming for resolutions.
Furthermore, I'm fed up with the way the greedy 1 percent treads on my constitutional rights!
That said, I have a plan!

The main goals of *Keep Voting, America* are to encourage US citizens to gather the family together, go unplugged, talk *with* one another, and study how the United States survived for nearly 250 years. Follow these ideals for one hour each week, and steady as you go. Can do? Most notably, maintain your voting status.

A meeting of the minds will continue your cooperation to live in peace and prosperity for those who *value* liberty. Follow the outline in *Keep Voting, America* and start relearning how our government has maintained liberty for all. But then, if you feel that liberty is not essential, I encourage you to continue reading so I may lay out a couple of ways your future liberties can play out in a positive light.

In the text are oodles of questions to ponder and many likely pursuits in which you can get involved. Heck, I lost count of how many I offer to guide your interest toward continuing the wisdom of our country's creators.

If you choose to continue reading this book, your patriotic side will become insightful while crewing your family political ship. There may be rough weather ahead, and the liberty ship might develop stress fractures and take on water. As Winnie-the-Pooh would say, "Oh, bother!" Navigate through the pages in *Keep Voting, America* to find ways to patch up the leaks and maintain a steady course as you sail through the stormy conditions ahead. When the calm seas draw near, take time to enjoy smooth sailing. Talking with one another helps you realize the inalienable rights that our country's founders gave us are for *everyone—forever!*

As an average voting citizen, I am bewildered at the US big corporations', bank executives', and politicians' *unwillingness* to clean up the air I breathe and the water I drink! But I need help from the country's core citizens—the families.

Okay, let's strike a bargain. Continue reading this and other books about our country as you go unplugged and talk *with* your family to stop the demise of our liberties. Are you willing to invest some of your precious time to improve your quality of life? Shall we embrace within this bargain the wealthy? Maybe the rich folks will consider developing a conscience while taking part in the process! The possibilities are real.

Recall the words mentioned earlier—*furious, screaming, fed up*, and *I have a plan*. If your impression of the status quo doesn't work anymore, your next port-of-entry is where you start your engines.

*Start reading!*

The United States Family Liberty Plan is a guide to aid in the establishment of your exceptional Family Political Council.

A colleague of mine in my local English reading tutor program asked if I could sum up this book in twenty-five words or fewer:

Within *Keep Voting, America* are copious accounts of our country's trials and tribulations. Gather your family, and talk politics with one another and me!

Notes and dates recorded: As you go through *Keep Voting, America,* you will find several blank pages with the phrase, "Notes and dates recorded." You, the Head of Household (HH), are encouraged to use these pages as an organizational tool for your journal.

# WELCOME ABOARD THE *SS INCENTIVE*!

Step one: By purchasing this book, you have completed your first action toward becoming a more valued, honest, and trustworthy US voting citizen. Not enough of an incentive? How about improving your quality of life?

Step two: Read chapters 1 through 9 to gather a few tools for your unique Family Political Council. It's a big step, but for the sake of expediency, take one to two weeks to do this before moving on to the next step. Do you need a third incentive? Why is *unearned* income not taxed?

Step three: Read chapters 10 through 22, where you will find a plethora of activities at which each family citizen can become skilled while everyone's awareness matures. (Easy does it—choose one or two activities at a time per citizen.) How about a fourth incentive? Preserve the freedom to worship as you wish.

Step four: In chapters 23 through 27, discover what the future can embrace! And as for the next incentive, consider keeping parks clean, open, and well illuminated.

Step five: Follow along to the appendices, using them as resources and a road map. Need another incentive? Slow down the rising cost of education!

Now, it's your turn to explore your own incentive for getting involved.

I encourage your family to test this plan for one month.

# INTRODUCTION

My New Year's resolution for 2010 was to reread the Constitution of the United States of America. I graduated from high school several decades ago, and ever since then, I hadn't so much as looked at the document, let alone studied it. I began a natural process of research: one document after another, one story after another, and one magazine article after another. My enthusiasm to feed this newfound patriotism was growing. I also watched a television program called *Liberty's Kids* that roused my desire to write down my thoughts on government. *Maybe I could write a book on politics*, I thought. But what tack would I take? Who would want to read a book on politics? Then I thought about the liberties we Americans are losing and decided I had to do something because turning a deaf ear to the calamities involving my quality of life was upsetting me. My focus became the driving force to write *Keep Voting, America*.

After mustering the courage, my first step was to seriously look at what is going on in my country today. What I discovered was *not* to my liking. Americans, we are at serious risk of losing our liberties—and we are doing it to ourselves. What could one voting citizen do to stop the demise of our free world? Reading my notes, I began thinking of ways I could help get back our liberties. And then, I took the second step; I started writing in earnest.

As my research continued, I kept finding other avenues to pursue. Ideas like family treasured teachings and the many different cultures here in the United States. And then, moral issues came front and center as I contemplated our liberties demise at the hands of special interest's groups from greedy individuals to lobbyists. Politics and morals proved to fit into my blueprint for *Keep Voting, America* as I developed this guidebook bringing about the United States Family Political Plan. We, the US voting citizens, have to get started rekindling our patriotic sides *immediately.*

In my search, I came up with one disturbing entity that stood out from all the devices man has created: the cell phone. I'm referring specifically to the spell that cell phones have on people. I do not advocate abolishing this handy tool. More to the point, I heard about the "go unplugged" concept and derived a plan to create a guidebook for the United States Core Citizen: the family. Each family will get together once a week for one hour in their home (a safe place) to talk *with* one another, with all communication devices turned *off.* My third step was naming this gathering the Family Political Council. Family members are now council citizens. They will sponsor debates, hold offices, vote on propositions, work out any personal problems, and even consider volunteering; there is so much work to be done. The fourth step is to have the council study our country's past, present, and future government. As all this transpires, we will have voters informed and ready to take back the running of this country. You have this right!

Whatever you do, please stress good communication skills among council citizens. And be professional about using the English language. Steer clear of ambiguities by getting the facts right.

I hope you find harmony and laughter as you sail your council ship through life's journey.

I was a Mariner during my High School years of Girl Scouting, therefore, you will find several references to nautical terms.

Notes and dates recorded:

# AUTHOR'S MESSAGE

The text is not in the form of a cut-and-dried lesson plan. Rather, I chose to add special touches, like little known facts about people who shaped our country, a plethora of questions, alerts, subjects to ponder, and even a sprinkling of humor.

The main idea behind the Family Planning Council is to set aside a time and place void of distractions to go unplugged once a week and talk politics with one another. What a concept! Why would a family want to spend quality time together? A couple of important reasons would be to gain a better quality of life and to strengthen the family's resolve. This can be accomplished by doing the following:

A. holding weekly councils called (your family name) Political Council—You, the head of the household, are the one to locate a secure environment in your home to accommodate all family members. Pick a room large enough so everyone can be comfortable. Practice good posture while you participate in your council. Next, set the time and day to meet, designating between one and two hours maximum.
B. get in the habit of associating freely
C. develop trust worthy citizens through your council while studying the following documents and many other publications, public and private:
   - the Articles of Confederation
   - the Declaration of Independence
   - the Constitution of the United States of America
   - the Bill of Rights through the Nineteenth Amendment
   - Abigail Adams's letter to her eleven-year-old son
   - the writings of Elizabeth Kate Stanton
   - actions by Cesar Chavez for farm workers
   - self-help books on running a household efficiently
   - plus a surplus of documentaries

Rule one: be respectful when speaking.

This book includes many suggested activities and a profusion of foregone conclusions. It's enough to overwhelm anyone with a sane mind-set. Therefore, work with only one or two ideas at each council. It is important for all core citizens to get started now, allowing each council the time to work through the issues facing the voting citizens. The aim is to do this before your liberties are gone.

If you are following my nautical theme, consider entering the council chamber as the navy personnel boards a ship. Ask the OD (Officer of the Deck or, in our case, mayor or head of the household), for "Permission to come aboard, sir (or ma'am)." Just a thought!

## Money talks, too bad politicians are listening

When too many US citizens are reluctant to get involved with governing the country, we all suffer ongoing deceit from current government trustees. In this context, wouldn't it mean political office holders working on our behalf—you know, the voting US citizens? Dozens and dozens of investigative reporters and documentaries have painted a perverse picture of how government agents, in the past as well as today, are in business for themselves and their money promoters. The "Open for Business" sign seems to beckon private donors like CEOs of wealthy companies, PACs, and bank executives to pull on the candidates' purse strings, securing financial and political paybacks.

## Speaking of election costs

For the candidate to get elected to office, in most cases, he or she will have to borrow funds to pay for all the TV time needed to broadcast commercials. And that, my friend, turns out to be a costly endeavor, usually to the tune of millions of dollars. The 99 percenters like you and I don't have the mega bucks needed to help our candidate get elected to national, state, and local offices.

Even in the smaller political arenas, buckets of greenbacks or Bitcoins are necessary to elect, say, the city dogcatcher. Unfortunately, we need trained and compassionate animal-control experts. There are too many people abusing their cats and dogs and causing strife in their neighborhoods, which, I might add, are made up of a whole bunch of us—citizens as well as a full barnyard of critters. The government needs to step in, curtail the abusers, and get our four-legged friends out of harm's way. Our loving tail wagers don't deserve the abusive people who disregard the welfare of domestic animals—hence the necessity of the city dogcatcher to alert the perpetrators to the fact that our society will not tolerate bad behavior toward animals. Next thing you know, we all show up in the overcrowded courtrooms.

It is hot and steamy—a tin of sardines comes to mind. Fines are levied; maybe jail time is handed down. What a total waste of our time, taxes and the unnecessary suffering forced on our precious, obedient, canine companions.

Now that we have taken care of our house pets, what about the obligation a public office holder has toward the people? And who are these people? For one, ill-informed American voters who elected the candidates into office are some of these people. At least the voters fulfilled their duty to the country. Second, with regret, we must include those who *chose* not to vote. What about the citizens who no longer register for the vote? And most disturbing is those registered voting citizens who were demoralized and kept from voting!

*All US citizens have the right to vote their conscience—period!*

Admission to the political theater is *not for sale*. The entry fee is a majority vote on Election Day. Well, the popular vote is questionable. The general voting citizen sometimes feels that his or her vote won't make a difference and is discouraged from voting. Let me be perfectly clear on this topic: the *money* people (such as political PACs backing their choice of candidate) are not the majority. For the typical minority citizens, the 1 percenters, you can bet these money people are going to throw money around and hoodwink the general voting population into voting for the money people's candidate. And, their money probably doesn't have a picture of George Washington on the face. Sometimes, I feel tricked. No wonder most citizens don't want to talk politics.

Let's take a moment to look at the word *politics*. The word has *polite* as its base; a polite person conveys thoughtful attention and proper behavior. This is a far stretch from the people sitting on the city council, as well as your neighbor who demonstrates in public his or her uncaring, crude behaviors. While we are at it, the word *civil* means being just polite enough to not be rude. People use this type of communication too often. Later, much to their vexation, the unthinking citizens will have to justify their poor choice of words. Rudeness is expressed too easily; watch a couple of reality shows if you don't know what I mean. The latest arena is the internet. What a waste of time. Let's play nice and be polite, be thoughtful, and most of all carry on a *meaningful* dialogue. That said, let's get back to the big bucks.

Election Day is over (*Keep Voting, America* was written during the 2016 election fiasco). The new government leaders are now pressured to covertly pay back the campaign dollars that got them into office. They do this by means of passing legislation on behalf of—you guessed it—the select few campaign supporters. Thus, the elected officials leave the rest of the population in the dust. And *they know it!* In my town, the council citizens approved a contract for a landfill construction project right next to one of the town's rivers that supplies 20 percent of our drinking water. The headlines read, "Landfills Leak!" Guess who got the contract? The out-of-towners who supplied the campaign money guaranteeing a councilperson's seat at city hall. And who is supposed to pay for this unwanted landfill? Every taxpayer in my town. Adding insult to injury, our tax money will probably leave the state. The taxpaying town folks will be left holding the leaky bag. No wonder government budgets are insufficient to run the city. But there is a shining light to this tale: we the voters finally eliminated the landfill request coming from our city council. There is no more threat to our drinking water—for now.

How did the candidate and the out-of-town money people form an alliance? Could the element of greed be uniting this bunch?

Another of my goals for writing *Keep Voting, America* is to assist Americans in securing transparency in government. Per the Constitution, the power to run our government was placed in the hands of the voters as guardians while Congress is in session. But lately, we are compelled to embrace so many changes in every conceivable direction that it's nearly impossible to understand what the politicians are doing. Transparency? Sleight of hand? Maybe too many chefs are adding too many rules and regulations to the political pot, making the political soup boil over. And there is more: trying to maneuver through the undecipherable legalese in the voting pamphlets requires a law degree when trying to make head or tails out of all those propositions on Election Day. Many voters feel like folding up their tents and moving out of town—or the country.

I imagine a conversation with you, the head of the household, going as follows:

*Author:* "Do *you* have an attorney on retainer?"
*HH:* "No."
*Author:* "I didn't think so. Neither do I. Can you see any parallel to a top-heavy government?"
*HH:* "The picture is getting clearer."
*Author:* "I know I am bewildered by the tomfoolery generated in government."
*HH:* "Tomfoolery in government? How did we get to this state of affairs?"
*Author:* "Too many citizens felt they didn't have the time to govern this country."
*HH:* "That's how I felt. And I thought my vote didn't count."

*Author:* "Oh, but you are heard when you vote. Create your Family Political Council, go unplugged for one hour each week, become politically proactive, and set an even keel toward making a shift away from a top-heavy government with no transparency to a government by the people with full disclosure."

*HH:* "I can see family, friends, neighbors, and even coworkers getting together and talking with one another to work up enough courage to step into the polling booth and know we have been counted! In the past, I have only voted for the presidency and glazed over the propositions."

*Author (with a smile):* "Thank you for listening to me!"

There will be no United States Core Citizens' conventions or PACs organized. Simply put, the American family following the go-unplugged council guide has the potential to gain a better understanding of how the country is run and to reclaim quality of life through their actions, all the while keeping the politicians in check.

*Hesitation is too high a price to pay if we are to secure the future of our freedoms.*

## Something ominous

Misinformed citizens are willing to shut down the government for economic reasons. This is awful! Failing to recognize the overall cost of such actions could damage our nation's economy more than what has already happened—lost jobs, lost tax revenue, lost freedoms, increased crime levels, and unsafe working conditions like those our country experienced during the Prohibition and the Great Depression. A question comes to mind: How many government departments are necessary, and why are they necessary? Exactly what are our tax dollars being used for? Landfills? Guns and training in Syria? Lobbyists? Overwhelmed?

## But there's more

What about the increasingly outdated infrastructure? Instead of purchasing a four-hundred-dollar toilet, we could redirect that money toward our perilously decaying bridges. Lost wages, unsafe bridges, and advertisers urging us to live high on the hog, so to speak, cannot endure. Now just a minute—isn't it true that spending money fuels our economy? We must buy, buy, and buy some more. Round and round we go!

Unfortunately, governing the United States has become a shaky tightrope for regular citizens to traverse. Too many acrobats could snap the overburdened wire, setting up a domino effect that will nullify the work done and cost the 99 percenters more and more money in taxes. And for what? Shall we make repairs or buy another four-hundred-dollar toilet? Repairs are boring, and toilets that flush with no hands are more sensational.

Are regular citizens purchasing government bonds for expensive toilets? Or does that money go for fees and penalties due to the bridge repair delays? Are there enough regular people buying bonds to possibly reverse our national debt? That would be nice. Are some of these people from foreign countries? How much of America do they own? Foreigners don't give a damn about our liberties! But let's get back to the crumbling bridges washing away in a flash flood. The saying "Can't get there from here" holds a whole new meaning in this context. *I feel ill!*

Hold on. In good faith, the Constitution tells us we are a nation governed by the people.

*Keep Voting, America,* along with other reading materials, will help direct families toward a better grasp of how the United States has evolved through the centuries. Read and discuss in your council possible ways to veer politicians away from their hell-bent, arrogant attitudes, especially regarding things like gerrymandering election districts and denying the voters' freedom to write in a candidate's name of their choosing. We must understand that taking away our write-in choice of candidate is a direct strike against democracy.

In 2016, the voters of Hong Kong demonstrated against Mainland China because their freedom to write in their choice of candidate had been taken away. This drama will play itself out in time. As a US voter, I can only hope that Hong Kong voters will win out.

For many citizens, voting is a guessing game. As your council progresses, a satisfying benefit for the family will manifest in the form of confidence when entering the voting booth on family council, city, state, and Federal Election Day—and not just in the election year evenly divisible by four but in every primary election. Familiarity with the issues takes the guesswork out of which squares get your mark. The family voting citizen can conduct business when everyone knows both sides of each concern. I offer stacks of possibilities throughout the six components in *Keep Voting, America* for you to build your awareness of what you can do, government agencies to contact, a list of supplies to help you as you go unplugged for an hour once a week and talk with one another.

## Willing to roll up your sleeves

The abusive powers being exploited by public servants cannot exist when the citizens are knowledgeable, willing to roll up their sleeves, discussing the issues, and then voting on the issues. In this context, rolling up your sleeves means offering to work on a task and then, if needed, amending the status quo.

We need to be active stewards in government. We must fire and replace the overpaid, lackluster politicians and any city, county, state, and federal employees. In my opinion, there are too many government employees; they need to be gone! This is a scary proposition since I'm advocating the growing occupancy of the unemployment line. And it's easy for me to say—I'm retired.

Many folks are finding their own employment through entrepreneurship. But I must caution those who do this to make it legal. We US citizens will regain full liberties for our efforts. Elect to keep in mind all the wasteful spending, and then the betrayal of US citizens will diminish.

Basically, voting citizens have a natural ability to make honest decisions. Following the procedures in *Keep Voting, America* will help family citizens heighten their proficiency in recognizing what path to take while gaining a better understanding of what is expected of them. Getting involved in the government from the local city council through national Election Day validates governing by the consent of the governed. Don't let the politicians usurp your powers. So far, the people of the United States of America can choose, among other things, the following:

- religious preference
- dream job
- place of residence
- to save or spend hard-earned money (I recommend saving)
- to attend the college of their choice, or not attend
- to use their constitutional right to speak freely
- to go about their lives without fear of government domination

I'm adding to this list one more element: you can exercise these liberties if you do not harm me or anyone else in the process. Here's a thought: let's *debate* what liberty means to each one of us. As Americans, we have the ability and the right to make our dreams come true. Our Constitution set the stage for permission to, among other activities, make ourselves happy and prosperous, speak out against the rogue government, work for a large or small company, and even work for ourselves. Simply put, without liberty, we *lose* what it means to be an American!

Through the US Constitution and the Bill of Rights, our Founding Fathers guaranteed us liberty. If we are to continue government of, for, and by the people, we must be informed, be partners in our government, and be vigilant!

If you choose not to get involved, the alternative is anarchy. The results of that are no more dreams, no more hopes, no more liberty, no more nut'n!

What benefits would you like to have? Use the space below to note them, but be careful what you wish for!

My list of benefits are:

## Absenteeism

Let's take a moment to look at these two words: *absentee landlord*. If you're familiar with the term, then you know what happens to a property located hundreds of miles, even in a different county, from where the landlord lives—decay, equipment failure, illegal activity, and so on. Because of the landlord's absence, she or he doesn't know that things are going terribly wrong, causing extensive damage that will cost the landlord thousands of dollars to fix, not to mention lowering the property values of the neighborhood.

Substitute an absentee landlord with the US citizen choosing not to vote. One glaring difference between these two scenarios is that the citizen lives close to where she or he votes. Enter the absentee ballot. You can't get any closer to the polling place than from your living room to the mailbox. Or maybe the citizen isn't sure whether to vote yea or nay for a judge to be seated on the bench and then doesn't bother to vote. And now we pause for a commercial message: Go unplugged, *form* your Family Political Council, and talk *with* one another about the issues printed on the forthcoming ballot!

Excellent, you are ready to vote intelligently. You might encourage your schoolchildren to bring home their social studies current events work and discuss the issues during council. This is where you, the parent, can help your kids learn the rudiments of *thinking*—and at the same time sharpen your own personal thinking skills. Comprehending current affairs is an activity the entire family council can share in. What joy! By the end of the week, your kid might just get an A, if that's the kind of results desired when learning new things. But make this a roundtable discussion and not a one-voice activity. For the citizens who are not in school, just because you are a high school graduate, or not, or you finished college, or didn't, don't stop learning. In fact, the newfound wisdom in adulthood is abundantly significant and continually uncovers additional clarity. Newfound knowledge promises a wealth of—well, anything, from amazing fun to a plethora of substantial discoveries throughout a person's life. If US citizens are to keep services like the public library bookmobile functioning for generations to come, voters must keep bringing to light all aspects of how America evolved throughout the past two and a half centuries. Not just the wars and not just what you want to remember—*all* US history.

As US citizens, we have the right to all the following:

- vote with our feet
- tell Congress to stop fiddle farting around

- read what we want to read—a few pictures are okay, but let's keep it socially mindful
- have quality of life (I didn't say quantity)
- own property whether we are female, of African ancestry, or naturalized citizens
- work for a promotion using honest, diligent work habits
- legally protest peacefully without reprisal
- be tried by a jury of our peers (we need a dialogue on this topic)

## Who owns America?

It bothers me a little when a foreigner, not a citizen of the United States, can own property on American soil. Are they held accountable for what they do with their property? Did our government officials pave the way for foreigners to buy up our land? I'm sure the desire for mega bucks is at the root of these transactions, for both buyer and seller. But how interested are the foreigners in our liberties? The same can be said about Americans buying property in foreign lands.

To sustain freedom, it is imperative that we pay attention to the way government is run. Show Congress that we only *loaned* the power to them. In turn, Congress will assist us while governing the nation. Get into the habit of writing and sending meaningful letters and e-mails.

All voting US American citizens owns the United States!

Notes and dates recorded:

# UNIT ONE

# CHAPTER 1

Mentally prepare for your Family Political Council

*Keep Voting, America* is an unfinished work because I want to allow some wiggle room while setting up your family council. We begin with the foundation for the head of household, or HH.

## In the beginning, we...

Start the process by reading through chapter 4. In the text, I talk about three main lifestyles, starting with the extremes: (1) the person following a hectic timetable and (2) the person with too much time on his or her hands. Of course, there is the middle group of people who is not sure where their priorities lie and figure they don't have time to get involved with community activities. Whichever lifestyle you identify with, you, the HH, might enlist the help of a family citizen or a close friend as you collect the few items necessary for your first council.

The three life styles are as follows:

1. The tightly knit family, already enjoying the ability to talk freely with one another, will hit the floor running as they start the process of relearning how the government was intended to work for *all* its citizens.
2. Some families will progress slowly in order to allow time to bring everyone to the table, literally.
3. Thinking of prioritizing their lives is seemingly impossible.

I believe all citizens need to come to grips with the demise of our vanishing freedoms. In less than one generation, this nation could conceivably parish. Start your own unique Family Political Council and talk with one another about your personal and political successes and failures. We have a good thing going here in the United States. Let's not lose it!

The prep work should take about one week but no more than two weeks. After collecting a few items and some knowledge of *Keep Voting, America,* bring the family together, display the tools at the first council, and include books you have on hand.

Keep your spending subdued until your council establishes a budget. Things work better when you put in the effort.

Later, you can check your local library and the internet for more reading materials like *The Separation of Church and State*, edited by Forrest Church—a worthwhile read.

Now that I have retired, I'm not a hurry-up-and-get-it-done kind of gal. However, as to the running of our government, things have got to change quickly. Keep in mind that the highest priority is to bring the *whole family* together to talk about ways each citizen can improve his or her personal life. A second matter is learning little-known US history in order for Americans to avoid an oppressive way of life. Third, invite family, assemble your first council, and then continue reading through chapter 9. Once your council is started, you and your helper can start reading chapter 10. This can help you stay slightly ahead of your council's progress. The chief concepts of *Keep Voting, America* are basically two-fold:

- Follow the guidelines and work through the personal issues blocking each citizen's path before the problems become awkward or overwhelming. It is plausible that the entire family will reap many benefits beyond whatever efforts they bring to the table!
- In tandem, assist your family toward tracking the US political journey from the seventeenth through the twenty-first centuries. It's a tall order, but involvement from all Family Political Council citizens has the potential to make your once-a-week council meaningful and lasting. Please put literature and films on war at the bottom of the list of study.

Continued journeys in the family political ship won't guarantee your family a "happily ever after"—that's for fiction writers. However, a key benefit for council citizens is having the potential to gain insight in the voting process within the family as well as the greater society. Your family's actions can pave the way for a better quality of life. What remains? However slight your commitment is, engaging your time and effort in an orderly fashion will pay off in spades. Claim your power to keep programs like the public library bookmobile gassed up for its trips to locations all around your town. I mention this because my city council tried to do away with this service, but the citizens in my town stopped them. Keep in mind that if the politicians do not listen to the people or respond in kind, the citizens can activate the powers for action to vote the politicians out of office. All US citizens with suffrage have this right. Later, I suggest going online to research how citizens can vote a politician out of office. It's an interesting process. Use caution, this must not become a 'witch hunt'.

As the HH, you will be setting the stage for family members to make wise decisions on Election Day. Think of it this way—by going through this process, you will become better informed. Being informed beats the heck out of ignorance, hands down!

At the end of the fourth or fifth council, discuss your expanded knowledge and how the family feels about your council's development. Next, vote on whether you want to stay with the weekly family quality times together while continuing to study past and present governing actions or set the council adrift without a paddle. Whichever way the wind blows, your efforts will prove that you have the conviction to complete your probationary period, marking your council time as a substantial accomplishment. Consider this: if nothing had been ventured, then you would have gained absolutely nothing. So feel good about your success.

*Suggested Action*: Adopt the United States Family Liberty Plan so that each US citizen will possess the stuff of influence to quietly and powerfully arrest the demise of our disappearing inalienable rights. (See the word *inalienable* defined in A8.)

- First, make a conscious decision to stop blaming everyone other than yourself. But don't beat yourself up!
- Second, with the help of the procedures outlined in *Keep Voting, America*, all citizens can start to grasp a better understanding of the true meaning of liberty.
- Third, start a habit of voting in *all* elections: federal, state, local, and especially those of your Family Political Council. You might even consider running for a public office—*you have the right!*

Voting is an integral part of this plan.

## A few ideas to get you started retrieving our lost liberties

1. If you think the government is managed unjustly, then … *you* do it?

So, you think I'm off my rocker? Oh, but I'm serious. We, the taxpaying US family core citizens, including the single citizens, have the right to run this great country. The Constitution tells us so. But how do we do this individually or in unison?

- Start thinking of where improvements can be made in your personal life, like developing a healthy food plan or cleaning out that unused room for your round-table discussions.
- Next, think of community improvements with which you can get involved. Take baby steps at first; there are boatloads of community projects out there needing your support, like beach cleanups.
- For now, put world peace aside, please. It's just a teensy-weensy tad out of reach. The United States Family Liberty Plan encourages council members to oversee the governing of the United States. But first, let's start with the local and remarkable governing body of *your family.* By becoming active in your Family Political Council, you will generate the opportunity to guarantee council citizens the fulfillment of the American Dream.

As a side note, I don't believe the phrase "achieving the American Dream" is in our Constitution. So what freedoms *are* in our Constitution? Could it be that we, the everyday voting citizens, have the right and duty to govern our country through the vote? Do we own the guarantee for each citizen to experience quality of life? When we understand these concepts, then and only then can we answer the ultimate question: What does the American Dream hold for me and my family?

Remember the saying "A chain is only as strong as its weakest link"? Elevating citizens' awareness of how our government is run will affirm our political chain sound as well as robust, today and into the future.

## 2. Suggested possibilities

Before we get to the core of the matter, may I make two suggestions? First, allow me the opportunity to offer you a starting point for recovering US citizens' inalienable rights. Citizens within the family and the greater community are entitled to the following:

- a good education
- the ability to cross state lines without having to carry a passport
- quality of life, such as paved roads without potholes
- freedom to dream the impossible dream
- a host of other uplifting pursuits

Second, follow the step-by-step instructions to begin your own (Family name) Political Council. Try this plan; it beats the alternatives!

Please set aside any negative feelings you might have toward Washington, DC. Instead, give this proposal serious consideration for the possibilities instead of saying, "It's too complicated!" or "You want me to ponder what's going on at city hall?"

The benefits of developing your own Family Political Council are huge. We can carry out many beneficial activities:

- making changes for citizens, franchised or not, and not just for corporations, bank executives, and career politicians
- upholding freedom of speech
- limiting terms of every office—federal, state, city, your council—making it possible for more citizens to step up to the podium and experience firsthand the running of our country (you do have this right)
- US citizens with feet planted here decreeing their right to vote

While establishing your Family Political Council, I realize it might be difficult to get everyone on the same page, so to speak. Do your best by demonstrating good examples. They will come!

3. Uncertainty, working together, missing out

The council plan will soon be revealed. But first, choose the family phrase that comes closest to your own.

> d. The American family struggling to get along with each other—uncertainty.
> e. The American family cooperating as a unit—working together.
> f. The American family fractured and missing out altogether.

Then follow the guide below to work toward a good-natured family life. Bear this in mind: antisocial activities, illegal activities, and hateful subjects expressed inside your home *will* follow you out into the public. And that goes for Las Vegas, too! After all, you don't want to have a slip of the tongue and expose a deep, dark secret when casually talking with your neighbor. Maybe bring yourself toward changing your way of visualizing how you fit in the home, community, and other arenas. Evoke the concept of transparency; it's what we are aiming for.

Following are suggestions for possible actions in each family category.

> a. *The Struggling Family:* Examples in the text might impact families guardedly or unfairly. But don't let any citizen's misunderstandings

detour you. I implore a responsible family member (grandparent or teenager or any age in between) to do these tasks:

1. Gather a few supplies and only some understanding of the Constitution.

2. Encourage each family member to pick a subject he or she feels ardently about, whatever rains on their parade, and craft at least one solution. Some examples are financing the repairs on a bicycle, why children must be kind to their siblings, what can be done about the neighbor's barking dog, or why family members must make their beds every day. I heard that making your bed every morning helps keep your day in a positive light. I tried it and it works – on a subconscious level! At your third or fourth council, have each citizen speak for no more than ten minutes on the results they found through reading or talking with others. Be considerate of the time limit; we are not writing a ten-volume encyclopedia. There should be no pushing and no value judgments. Think of this as a democracy instead of a dictatorship.

3. In case your family members need to lift their spirits, I suggest this activity: talk about putting a fresh coat of paint on the front door, vote on it, and then do it. What a wonderful sense of pride your family can enjoy. I painted mine yellow! The goal is to make ready the commitment to carry out positive-minded duties, beginning at home.

4. After the family citizens start functioning in good faith, study can begin on the United States and how it evolved as a nation—the good and the bad. I must confess this is a tall order! But when all family citizens offer a bit of their time and effort, all sorts of wonderful things can be accomplished. This segment of the American population holds volumes of potential for the outstanding citizens yet to be discovered. Can you imagine running for governor of your state? Ooh! Chills! Be careful not to dwell on the negative.

b. *The Cooperating Family:* To start, follow the examples in this book by asking the family citizens to prioritize the different household duties within your home, significant or not—from emptying the trash to paying the rent or mortgage on time. This may sound simplistic, but discussing these chores during council meetings can show young children what their parents do to keep the house functioning well. Transparency is the goal! Keep it simple. A potential next step is to tackle the greater community, which will require a little more effort. One possible path the family can ponder is to research different local community action groups and vote on the one your family would like to support. One word of caution: there are countless community groups that will tempt each family member—some legal and some not so much. Finding a fit for the whole family could turn into a struggle of which the victor is the fittest, or loudest. One solution is to debate, but keep the debate civilized. Take into consideration that achieving world peace is outlandishly daunting and is of low priority for your family to take part in at present. As members of your Family Political Council, your family's objective is to become active, accountable citizens. Your aim as HH is to set an example for all the family citizens. Again, this is a democracy, not a dictatorship. You may soon learn to enjoy the coming together of differing ideas, but the subjects must be grounded in facts and honesty!

c.  *The Fractured Family:* This family yearns for any kind of family life. You, as a responsible family member, the HH, might approach a responsible member of the community to help you read *Keep Voting, America*. Maybe a teacher, the school nurse, or even a neighborhood police officer can fill this role (see note below). Talk with this person about the possibility of continuing with your Family Political Council. (Your enthusiasm to start this program may be contagious, so make sure your candidate is not overburdened already.) Who knows? This person might agree to be your acting judge! (More on the judge later.) You only need to ask. Don't give up asking until you find the right person who will be delighted to offer his or her assistance. A good fit for your family is paramount.

*Note:* When you approach potential candidates, talk about your intention toward starting such an adventure. Bring *Keep Voting, America* with you to show where your inspiration comes from. Then ask. They can only say yes or no. If you get a negative response, politely thank them for their time. Be careful not to stumble and fall into an uncivilized attitude. Someday you might ask them to speak at a future council. You never know where life will take you.

When debating in council, make sure everyone is talking on the same subject, all the while respecting other citizens input. After watching a few talk shows on TV, I was mystified as to why I had bothered to waste my time. The interviewees responded to one another's remarks by upping their volume as everyone talked at the same time, even going completely off subject and defying any possibility of a meeting of the minds. It seems like these programs exist only as a place for people to vent their lack of understanding; there is no finality, only open-ended discontent. And any form of compromise is lost when too many different viewpoints, one on top of the other, render useless the attempt toward working things out. Keep in mind that there are at least two sides to every problem. Still, on behalf of TV programming, I realize that they work on a strict time schedule. But come on, guys! There has got to be a better product coming out of all that babble! Too many of us merely talk *at* each other. What's a body to do?

4. Mentally preparing for your first council

When you were growing up, did you know of a family holding regular weekly family gatherings to discuss things like the following?

- issues within the family
- city-wide activities
- local school board problems and events
- city ordinances affecting the street in front of your house
- what was learned while visiting the state capitol
- why the US Constitution was written

To my dismay, my father was a traveling salesman (spare me all the jokes) and was seldom home to have such gatherings around the kitchen table. Hopefully, after reading *Keep Voting, America,* you will not miss out on the vital conversations and actions with which your family can get involved.

Finding practical ways to efficiently overcome individual problems before they become insurmountable is well within your grasp provided you put in a bit of forethought and planning. Below are actions to consider:

- personal changes you want to make
- any subjects you want to ponder in council, be sure to make them pertinent and timely

- topics to research while perusing the internet
- taking a field trip to your local library to experience the real deal: *books*

Remember, unresolved issues might take time, so take baby steps.

As a historical side note, in the 1770s, the colonists were out-and-out criminals (traitors, if you like) plotting against the king of England. Among the colonists, some wanted freedom from oppression, while others were happy to live under the king's protection. The Founding Fathers fought a war and wrote documents for freedom so US citizens could govern themselves. Article 5 tells us there is no limit on changes we can make in our government. That's powerful and precisely what we have been doing for close to two-and-a-half centuries. Well, at least some citizens have. All US citizens have the right to amend our laws—think Prohibition Era. Oops, bad example!

As to the protection issue mentioned above, it was *paramount* in the late eighteenth century to unite the thirteen colonies and form the federal government. This act announced to the rest of the world our ability to live in a *socially conscious government* and to be free from foreign domination. Our Declaration of Independence has been tested many times. At present, Americans are petrified; the threat against our free society is real. All citizens have an obligation to take up the cause, yet again, in order to retain our liberty. Your personal statement of belief, as you prepare for this journey, must include

| | | |
|---|---|---|
| *resolve, education,* and *courage* to be the guardians of liberty | ... not ... | guns, ignorance, and prejudicial hatred threatening the very life out of liberty! |

Americans, prepare yourselves to be part of the *solution!* And do this in the name of liberty everlasting.

Have I sufficiently sparked your wonderment to motivate you to gather the family, and maybe a couple of friends, so you can meet once a week, turn off all electronics, and talk politics with one another? Have you never taken the initiative to register to vote? Or are you aghast now that you realize your enthusiasm to vote has faded away? Why did you stop getting involved in the running of this country? Now is the time to step up to the mast with your family and friends, hoist those political sails, and navigate the rough winds of democracy. Remember that you are not alone; there are enough family and friends to crew your ship for liberty. If you need an extra hand, I would be most pleased to be added to your council.

Let's talk US politics and get on with improving our quality of life. Have you registered for the vote? If not, give me a call, and I'll procure a voter registration form for you and any other family members not yet registered.

Notes and dates recorded:

# CHAPTER 2

In the beginning, it is important to be prepared but not completely knowledgeable. Give your family a heads-up of your first council—up to one week, no more. At your first designated council, if not all citizens show up...be steadfast and hopeful the absent citizens will soon recognize the value in this new adventure. Make it clear that members in your family, including yourself, will be learning as the council progresses. In preparation for the initial council gathering, bring together the following or something similar:

- scraps of paper for handwritten votes
- journals for each citizen, with labels for each journal
- plenty of pencils and pens
- egg timer
- a rubber stamp that says "Approved" (or simply write it in black or blue ink)
- a Chinese gong or bell to announce the start of council meetings—be creative
- voter registration forms, official or your rendition of
- gavel or maybe a meat pounder, whatever you have on hand
- a dry erase board for an agenda, if you have one, or a printed or written-out agenda
- *Robert's Rules of Order*—in the beginning, check one out at your local library
- book of etiquette, from the library (remember to return these books in a timely manner)
- books on the writing of the Constitution (keep the number of books low for now)
- copy of the US Constitution in booklet form
- most important, bring fun to the process

Priority one is to observe the plan to go unplugged and talk *with* one another.


## Needing help?

Should the HH need help gathering everything, I suggest that she or he recruit help from another family member or a good friend. During your probationary period, I wouldn't include a homeless person wandering downtown. Maybe later you could set up an interview to hear such a person's point of view on politics; it could be interesting. Use caution and be sure an adult family citizen accompanies the citizens who are under the voting age. Don't be demanding—after all, this is a democracy. And do this in the light of the day, please.

## Becoming overwhelmed

It is prudent to realize that books written about our government documents could be biased; therefore, as you read, compare them with other publications. Manage your time so you won't become overwhelmed. Read for twenty minutes and then take a break. Step outside for a couple of minutes. Be sure to take an umbrella if it is raining or if the UV level is extremely high. Remember, take frequent breaks to avoid getting stuck reading words without understanding their meaning.

Notes and dates recorded:

# CHAPTER 3

To set up a detailed outline for the first council agenda, visit your city council chambers during session. As you compose your agenda, use key words. There's no need to write a long paragraph on each entry like I have done. In other words, it is not necessary to include all the grit and grim in your agenda.

## First council

A) Call to order on time! Arriving on time is vital, so handle this with the utmost concern along with turning off all communication devices. Do this willingly and with diplomacy.

    B) All citizens are to fill out voter registration forms, including the "mayor" and acting judge. (Information for the judge is in D section below.) If you can, pick up an application at the voter registrar office on the same day your city council meets. You can use the internet, but see if you can find the time to step into the registrar of voter's office. No pressure! Be prepared to utilize a citizen with suffrage to assist young children as they fill out the form. Be patient.

    C) Write a single paragraph about establishing a republic and descriptions for the duties of your public officers. In other words, the family council is to be governed by the family. Keep it brief. My suggestions: the mayor leads the council; a ways and means secretary (selected by the mayor), who will monitor the time limit for speakers and is responsible for all equipment used at the council, plus he or she will be the temporary registrar of voters, keeping the voter registration forms in a binder or a shoe box. A third officer is the recording secretary who is responsible for maintaining the minutes during the council, letter writing, and so on. Alternatively, the political offices could be councilperson, council treasurer, council planner, and others. Keep it simple; the goal here is to get council citizens thinking about what office they want to run for. You can discuss details of the political offices at the second council and then later agree to the duties for each office as you debate and then vote on them. The mayor is officially elected during the second council. Then, if the council wishes to continue the Family Political Council, all other political candidates are to begin running their campaigns starting around the fifth or sixth council. Also, be prepared to tutor the children in the political duties they might fulfill once your council votes to continue the FPC. Positions could be council page or animal control supervisor. Can't you just see how much fun you and the children will have during this process?

D) As for a judge, the HH makes inquiries for a senior member of the family, *not living in your home*, to act as temporary judge. A grandparent, uncle, or aunt who visits the family often can "sit on the bench." If such a person is not available, a wise and disinterested citizen who demonstrates good standing in your community might work. One example is the corner grocery store owner. Make sure you qualify him or her regarding availability. Try not to pick a popular person as he or she may not have the time to champion your endeavor. Prior to the initial council, instruct the stand-in judge to learn the basic duties and to prepare a five-minute talk on his or her qualifications. Your acting judge may want to watch a TV show such as *Judge Judy* for inspiration (minus the drama, please!). The stand-in judge is to be introduced at the initial council, at which time she or he gives the speech. During this council, the acting Judge is invited to register as a voting citizen. When judgments are to be made, the acting judge is solicited by letter or e-mail to appear in official attire (an official judge's robe). Maybe she or he can rent a robe for the day; it needs to be black. Perhaps, if you have an extended family member who sews and you are nice enough when asking, she or he might be happy to make the robe for your council. When it comes time to establish a permanent judge, the mayor will appoint a judge, and a unanimous vote of council citizens will be needed to ratify the appointment. The vote will be taken by a show of hands.

E) Check online for maps of your congressional district. It might be interesting to view a couple of congressional districts in another state as well. Some are extremely convoluted. Political parties have carved out oddly shaped voting districts resembling the fingers on your hand. Those sneaky politicians!

F) At all councils, have a copy on hand of *Robert's Rules of Order*. To ease your initial expenses, you may want to check out a copy at the library. Appoint a citizen to study along with you. For now, it's okay if you don't follow the protocol outlined in *Robert's Rules*. Learn as you go. But start this process early, you don't want to set up inappropriate habits.

G) First committee: appoint a two-citizen committee to come up with a couple of names for your council. One example is "Brooks Family of Five Political Council."

(Be sure to count the toddlers.) The committee members are to offer their suggestions at the second council for discussion and vote.

H) Among the many books on history, I suggest reading children's books; they are excellent for this research. Now, don't get your knickers in a twist. These books may appear naïve, but the text and pictures have merit. You might check on a film series written for television called *Liberty's Kids*. It gives an outstanding rendition of the turmoil in the late 1700s, even though it supports a Hollywood style of storytelling.

I) State that there will be a dress code. This is an official activity and warrants appropriate attire. Your first council will be exempted from this code. In other words, day wear appropriate for the office is desirable. It is not necessary to go under- or overboard with your dress code; bikinis are for the beach and formal attire is for state dinners. (Here's a thought: a formal "White House dinner" in your home might be a first-rate activity to hold in the future and an excellent excuse to dress up and use your best manners, fine china, and silver. But expensive items can wait until your treasury is substantial enough to budget money for such a robust expenditure. In the beginning, see if your Aunt Matilda will let you borrow her dinner set. Alert! It is vital to demonstrate, in good form, the handling of such fine china. Sending back chipped cups will *not* be tolerated. If you know a waiter or waitress, you might contract with them to serve your dinner. Keep the expense low but have fun. You all deserve it.

J) Introduce the concept of a quorum. When there is business to be done, in order for it to be legal and binding, a minimum number of council citizens must be present at every council. This is essential when a vote is called for. A quorum could be a total count of all citizens in your council or an agreed-upon percentage of that count. Discuss what a quorum is and then follow up with a consensus vote on the percentage. You just completed your first decree. See *Robert's Rules of Order*, 10th ed., p. 12, for more details. (A side note: I'm encouraging a little political license here because the number of office holders can, in some households, be the whole family. Some citizens may even have to wear more than one political hat.)

K) Discuss when and where your council sessions will take place—for example: Saturday at 5:00 p.m., lasting for one hour in the dining room, at which time the bell will be rung. All citizens need to be a little flexible when scheduling the council time and day. Once the council agrees, all citizens are to hold to it. A vote by show of hands of all citizens present is required straightaway and must be passed by a 100 percent majority. Make sure all citizens understand that this rule can, at a later date, be amended. Go easy at first.

L) All citizen's name will be printed or handwritten on the cover of his or her journal, including the citizens without suffrage. The mayor will ask all citizens to think of any personal concerns they may have and write it in their journal. There should be no pushing; each council member must decide for her- or himself. But make sure the concern is timely, for now we don't want to resurrect any monumental problems. But don't force the children—this is a democracy!

M) Ask for nomination for Mayor. Inform the candidates to write a five-minute campaign speech to be delivered at the beginning of the fourth or fifth council. Request the nominees keep a total of the money they spend for their campaign.

N) Ask for adjournment if there is no more business to be done.

I have laid out an ambitious undertaking; do your best and use some caution so you don't get caught up in overachieving. Do some brainstorming when solutions are needed. I suggest reading Benjamin Franklin's "Prudential Algebra" letter. Go online and key in Prudential Algebra. I've used his outline on many occasions and found my efforts were more than rewarding.

## A quick review of the plan's nuts and bolts before you continue

Before you start the first council, be sure you are ready to do the following:

- set aside an unplugged time and place to gather your family together to introduce the concept of the Family Political Council
- offer a single paragraph about establishing a republic within the family council to be governed by all family citizens
- encourage everyone to run for political office, enfranchised or not
- urge each citizen to write a brief note on one problem bothering him or her
- encourage each citizen to read books about the Constitution, letters written by our constitutional framers and their families, speeches made by regular people such as Elisabeth Katy Stanton, newspaper and magazine articles about the local projects affecting your family and neighborhood, and so on

Glance at appendix A9 for a short list of books published on the vast history of our country, but don't labor on it. You can tackle them later.

Be ready to

- inspire everyone to recognize all levels of government;
- settle disputes through a modest court system using a judge;
- encourage all citizens to attend the meetings on time and be appropriately dressed;
- demonstrate the skill of documenting what is necessary, leaving out the insignificant details (ideally, ask yourself if this subject is worth chiseling in stone);
- ask questions and more questions; and
- elevate citizens to volunteer for a committee to ink-out possible answers.

It's okay if your first councils appear imperfect.

Be sure you have the necessary equipment for the council:

- books and magazine articles about our Constitution—just a few for now
- copy of *Robert's Rules of Order*, a book on proper etiquette, and a thesaurus
- pens or pencils, journals, a registered-voter sign-in book (see appendix A3), voter registration forms (check with the registrar of voters office)
- secret ballot papers, a private polling place, and a box or hat to place ballots in
- a tape recorder other than a cell phone (optional)
- a gavel, a bell, and a timer—can be anything from an egg timer to a fancy Chinese gong

Have fun with this. But let's not have any obnoxious air horns. Let's refrain from blasting the family into the next county.

You might check your local library to see if they have books for sale. They have dirt-cheap prices.

**Rule two:** Actions and words having real merit is to be respected by all citizens during your Family Political Council!

Notes and dates recorded:

# CHAPTER 4

A condensed version of your first council's agenda

The following entries are not set in stone. Have fun with them!

1. call the council to order
2. voter registration forms
3. introduce duties of officers and call for nominations for interim mayor, appoint tutor for kids
4. introduce temporary judge
5. voting district maps
6. introduce *Robert's Rules of Order*
7. appoint first committee to come up with a name for your council
8. introduce possible reading list
9. dress code
10. quorum
11. determine week, day, and place for council
12. issue journals and assign citizens to enter a personal concern
13. ask for nominees for mayor, suggest nominees prepare campaign strategies for election on fourth or fifth council, keep record of spending
14. motion to adjourn

**Rule three:** Should any citizen of your council require a time out, it must be submitted in writing before the council and approved by the interim mayor.

The interim mayor will request that the recording secretary make appropriate labels for the journals with each citizen's name and title. The secretary can do this prior to the second council. For example, some labels may read "Citizen Roger," "Mayor Alice," "Recording Secretary Ben," "Ways and Means Secretary Bob," or "Judge Judy." Handwritten names and titles are okay for now, and the use of first names is okay because most of the citizens will have the same last name. We don't want to confuse the little kids.

One positive attribute at which the family can become skilled during council meetings is stated in James Madison's letter to Dr. Jacob de la Motta, August 1820. A partial quote is "mutual respect and good will among (all) citizens ... social harmony, and most favorable to the advancement of *truth*." For the most part, this is grossly missing in our congressional leaders as well as too many American citizens.

During a future council, request the citizen appointed to study *Robert's Rules of Order* to set up a study council. Request the council secretary to place it on the agenda for discussion among all citizens after the council votes to continue with the Family Political Council. Until the citizens have learned these rules, it will be okay to make errors in protocol.

For now, put this book aside and prepare to begin your Family Political Council.

~~~~~~~~~~~~~~~~~~~~~~~~~~~~~~~~~~~~~~~~~~~~~~~~~~~~~~~~

Notes and dates recorded:

# CHAPTER 5

I have laid out a lengthy agenda; therefore, write a brief agenda using key words from these two pages. Keep your thinking cap on as you work through this task.

## Second council

1. HH calls council to order, on time and names a temporary ways & means secretary and a recording secretary.
2. Have the council-naming committee introduce possible names, discuss, and vote.
3. All citizens are expected to be present, dressed for business, prepared, and *on time*. This is probably a considerable change to your everyday lifestyle, so take small steps until you feel comfortable with the new direction your family will be heading. Think of it this way: your council will last for only an hour or two a week. That's approximately 0.005 percent of your week. Piece of cake! But there should be no eating during council, please. And don't overdo the children's garments; they grow out of them so quickly. You might check out the vintage stores.
4. Assignment: Each citizen is to choose a public servant, present-day or historical, and write a brief journal entry about a political maneuver that candidate used to conduct his or her campaign for office. For this task, kids in middle or high school may want to pick a student who ran for a student body position.
5. HH makes these announcements preparing citizens for future councils:
    a. After voting to continue your political council: throughout the life of your council, all candidates are encouraged to campaign for mayor and other offices of your choosing.
    b. Be sure to keep an accurate account of the money spent on the campaign, if any. And absolutely no *bribes* will be accepted! Submit the account of your expenditures to the ways and means secretary
    c. Down the line, you might consider debating and writing legislative recommendations for future campaigns, like the maximum amount of money to spend on the campaign trail.

d. The interim mayor will request that the ways and means secretary make up a ballot for the first official vote. The ballot can be as simple as a sticky note for all citizens to write down his or her choice.

e. Later in your council, set up a committee to list a couple of questions for the candidates to debate. It should be interesting to see how the candidates handle the pressure.

f. Debate about a by-annual calendar date to hold elections and when to start the campaign.

6. The HH requests that the recording secretary write a letter officially inviting the judge to attend the fourth council, at which time he or she will hear the citizens' concerns and render a judgment. This is an official duty; therefore, the judge is expected to be dressed in a judge's robe at that council. Not every citizen will have a grievance to air at that council.

7. Address any new business.

8. Motion to adjourn the council, and so on.

**Rule four:** A debate, when arguing on just about every topic under the sun and beyond the stars squanders your time and energy. For our experiment, set your sights on relevant and timely topics to debate.

After your council votes to continue, consider electing a council page whose duties will include depositing official letters at the post office. This service industry is one nearing the reduction-in-force category. Better yet, save a stamp and hand deliver the letter. There is a renewed movement taking hold in America centered on cursive writing. Remember when you made circles and lines on lined paper? Your council would be a great environment in which to practice forming letters for beginners and grown-ups as well. We all need to improve our writing skills.

A do's and don'ts platform that you can follow within council

| Do | Don't |
| --- | --- |
| Keep an open mind | toss out new arguments or ideas |
| Look for joyful activities | Hold onto negative thoughts |
| Get into the habit of forward thinking | Dwell on the past |
| Respect yourself and others | Rain on others' parades |
| Practice honesty | Lie |
| Live a socially conscious life | Be an island to yourself |
| Be positive | Smother yourself with pity |
| Clean up your life | Trash your life |

Notes and dates recorded:

# CHAPTER 6

The following week, you might supply a pitcher of water—no bottles please—and enough glasses for everyone, using no paper or plastic except for your small children.

## Third council

1. Council is called to order *on time*.
2. HH calls on all citizens to give a ten-minute talk on what they have recorded in their personal journals about a political maneuver they read about or observed in person. Assist the small children with this task, but don't push.
3. Ask ways and means secretary to demonstrate the procedure for voting in their council. (place ballots alongside the sign-in book at the council's head table. (See Appendices A3 for sign-in book entries.) Include enough sharpened pencils in a small box so they won't roll off the table. Locate the polling place in a separate area, such as the living room. This may sound corny, but good habits are forming through your actions.
4. Until the children learn to write, they can sign with an X in the sign-in book. Teach them this is how illiterate people sign their names. In-order-to identify the X, the citizen teaching the children will write the child's name next to the appropriate X. (Later, the family may want to construct a real voting booth complete with a curtain as well as a slotted box to deposit ballots. Use your imagination and give it your best shot with the supplies you have on hand.
5. Announce: on the fourth or fifth council, each citizen will report a book or chapter he or she has read and the lesson learned; each citizen has ten minutes to talk. There should be no forcing in the beginning; ease into this part of your council. However, not being prepared for future councils is a different matter. Each citizen must be honest by sticking to the facts.
6. Ask if there is any further business, if none,
7. ask for an adjournment.

Note: For any of these instructions, the family has complete authority to make changes or create new details appropriate for their own council. However, the family must maintain the level of decorum described in *Robert's Rules of Order*. When making decisions, don't haggle too long over solving basic questions such as in which room the council will be held each week, as long as all citizens can sit comfortably (no lounging).

The mayor will establish subcommittees from time to time for various purposes, such as setting up a family council budget. The budget proposal committee will submit its findings at a future family council for debate and approval, where a consensus vote will be needed. The mayor will also appoint two citizens to visit the city council meeting. The delegates will report back to your family council about decisions that were made in the city council chambers. The mayor needs to set time limits as to when each subcommittee reports back to the Family Political Council. These subcommittees are where most of the work gets done.

**Rule Five:** If the council runs out of time, a postponement must be agreed upon with a majority vote of all citizens present.

All the above entries are important skills to employ in daily life, whether your council votes to continue after the probationary period.

Notes and dates recorded:

# CHAPTER 7

This is your most important council, and all citizens must be present.

## Fourth council

1. The council is called to order.
2. HH calls on each citizen to express his or her one concern – a grievance within the household. Limited to ten minutes, the ways and means secretary is to time each talk. Citizens talk directly to the judge, making final judgements – when necessary. Remember, *no finger pointing*.
3. HH calls for all mayor nominees to give their campaign speeches, hold to ten minutes.
4. HH calls a temporary recess until all citizens have voted. Have all citizens stand in line; sign in; vote in a separate room; return to council chambers, and drop secret ballots in a box or hat in clear view of all citizens. No snacks or meals are to be consumed unless there are extenuating circumstances.
5. After all votes are in, reconvene the council so the tally can be presented to the council citizens. The ballots will remain in the recording secretary's file, placed in a shoe box, or entered into a computer after council. Be creative. If possible, have one citizen, maybe your judge, observe the count. Then the recording secretary will announce the winner.
6. HH introduces the newly elected mayor to the council. The newly elected mayor thanks the HH as they transfer the gavel. If the two people are one and the same, well ham it up a bit! Mayor will now either appoint two secretaries or keep the ones the HH appointed.
7. The mayor asks for a motion to continue the council, and a second is called for. The mayor conducts a fifteen-minute discussion with all citizens on continuing the once-a-week unplugged times together. Next, the mayor invites each citizen to vote verbally one at a time. The recording secretary will call each citizen's name to vote yea or nay. If the vote is divided, the mayor will ask the citizens to debate their reasons for their vote, allotting two minutes for each person. (If a citizen does not take the full allotted speaking time, he or she may apportion the remaining time to another citizen. The ways and means secretary is to keep

accurate records of each citizen's time.) Now, a second vote is asked for that will hopefully establish a consensus. Either the council continues or the council is put into mothballs—think navy ships.

8. At this point, the mayor does one of two things:
   a. If the vote to continue fails, the mayor thanks the family for completing the experiment and sets in motion plans for a formal dinner to present the achievement certificate.
   b. Should the vote confirm the family's desire to continue their council, the mayor appoints a committee to start plans for a public celebration the following week.
9. The mayor asks for a motion to adjourn.

OK, this was monumental, so, everyone pat yourself on the back for a job well done!

**Rule Six:** No law-abiding citizen
is excluded from the council.

A formal certificate of completion is to be presented to the council citizens at a formal celebration, whether citizens vote to continue the council or not. Prior to this celebration, the mayor or a citizen who is savvy with computers can create a certificate of completion and hand deliver it to the secretary just before the council's celebration. If available, use a computer program for this purpose or ask at the office supply shop for a printed form. You might consider using a special calligraphy pen to fill in the council's name in the space provided. This is an important document, so be sure to finish it on time. (If your budget is tight, please don't go out and buy a special pen. A regular pen can do the honors.)

## Instructions for the recording secretary

When writing the minutes of each council, you only need to write key phrases. It is *not* necessary to write down every word uttered. When I was the interim secretary for my homeowners alliance, the president encouraged me to follow this approach for taking minutes. Boy, was I relieved. Some secretaries use an audio recorder in case they miss a detail.

Notes and dates recorded:

# CHAPTER 8

Unofficial fifth council: Brainstorming, a free exchange of ideas, and a work on truancy

Fifth or sixth council –

A. Call to order.
B. Mayor asks the recording secretary to take the roll of political officer's present and make an entry in the minutes.
C. Mayor introduces the concept of brainstorming – now the fun begins.....

If you need to have more time to plan your celebration, use this time for brainstorming. The policy for brainstorming is that no idea is a bad one. So all citizens are encouraged to fire out their ideas as the recording secretary writes them down on a white board, if you have one, so that all the citizens can see what is offered. Hold the brainstorming to no more than fifteen minutes. Everyone has the green light to dress casually because this is not a regular council. Now you are ready to plan your celebration and decide whom to invite as guests. During *this* session, acting outlandishly is *moderately* acceptable. Because there will be several decisions made at this council as you finalize preparations, truancy is not to be tolerated.

Excellence in forward thinking and positive actions are the order of the day. Make sure all citizens participate in this council. Try, I know you all are having fun, but, try to hold your cavorting to the specified one hour for council.

## Celebration council: One or two weeks later

At this celebration, the mayor requests that the recording secretary present the certificate to the newly formed political council citizens. All citizens are encouraged to sign the certificate. This completes the family's initial declaration of their Family Political Council. You might want to have a camera handy to record this event. Because of the "go unplugged" premise, use a camera instead of your cell phone. We don't want to get anyone in trouble. If you have the budget, you might sponsor a celebration; this will be a ceremony to remember. Plus, you will have witnesses to prove you accomplished your goal. However, if you chose to celebrate with your family in private, you might follow the state dinner idea.

## Failure to achieve consensus

Now, if for some unforeseeable reason there is no consensus to continue or halt the proceedings because of a missing or resistant citizen, the mayor may request a motion to recess until the following week for the following:

- Find out why the resisting citizen(s) did not agree with the rest of the council. (Remember this is not the Spanish Inquisition, so go easy on the poor soul.)
- Find out why the citizen(s) was not in attendance.
- Reach an amicable conclusion.

The mayor can ask the judge to officially preside over an additional council that can ferret out the reason the citizen chose not to be in attendance. Now, the Family Political Council is in limbo, which is not a comfortable place to be. At this council, the judge listens to all debates. Each council citizen has ten minutes to present his or her case.

*All* citizens are to attend. Because this council is all about debate, make it polite, informative, and "Just the facts, ma'am. All we want are the facts," as Joe Friday from the old TV show *Dragnet* used to say.

If your judge is unable to render a decision, the council will continue to be in recess. But once your judge makes a ruling, the mayor can then call for a vote. Remember, what you get back is dependent on what you put in. Hopefully, the concerns are cleared up in a timely manner and a final vote made to continue or eliminate your Family Political Councils. It's up to the entire council, maybe with a little help from Joe Friday.

Congratulations! You have completed your probationary period. Now, if you have chosen to disband the council, please feel good about your efforts to follow through with your preparations and completing the probationary period. May I suggest keeping this book on the shelf? You never know when the opportunity may present itself again in the future!

After the vote to continue, consider designing a formal letterhead for your stationery. If you have the budget for personalized stationery, I encourage you to invest in it. Letters that are typed or written in longhand hold more clout, especially when they are on professionally designed stationery. A clever council member could try his or her hand at designing a seal or logo using the council's name. Enjoy the process! (See appendix A10 for a suggested stationery letterhead design.) The rest is up to you on how to go about the business of your Family Political Council. Make sure you keep up your continued reading of US history as well as present-day political events, accomplishments, and even the behaviors of your elected officials. You might want to hold in your council a candidate-to-candidate Q&A session to help everyone determine which candidate (family member) gets his or her vote on your council's Election Day. Watch their body language as you listen to their responses. For now, keep your efforts focused on your city council and your Family Political Council.

Now that you are going to continue your Family Political Council, I suggest that you invite the following, provided the family is comfortable with the way you handle your council:

- extended family
- a local shop owner, maybe the baker who decorated your celebration cake
- a neighbor
- a person you know in the military
- a coworker starting the naturalization process
- friends
- maybe a local politician who would like to observe your adventure

A crucial element to be aware of in council is to avoid falling into the trap where only one or two citizens do all the work. Your journey will lose its luster if this is the case.

Notes and dates recorded:

# CHAPTER 9

An important message to all citizens

This is *not play,* nor is it a popularity contest. Rather this is a serious matter for which the council citizens unite together to do the following:

- establish the duties of the family political offices
- make judgments regarding any wrongdoing
- offer political and social education
- discuss salaries (see below) for each office as well as a budget to run your council
- levy and collect fines

Unit 2 discloses more details to guide you in future councils.

Salaries can be in the form of permission to have a party with friends, a meal at a favorite restaurant after council, and so on—be adroit! Perhaps a more substantial payment for the citizens still in school could be in the form of a savings account to mature upon their twelfth-grade graduation. Caution: there will be no tolerance of absconding with your children's savings accounts—*period!* This is a major offense, and the perpetrator is subject to a stiff penalty. Just in case you plan on speculating the funds, don't do what the US government did to the Social Security funds. Instead, try debating about what is important for each citizen in your family council, and then write legislation for salary options. This is where your family will build its resolve.

Make sure you find time for humor; it helps keep an even keel for your council's future destinations as you navigate through the political waters. After the vote for continuing your council, a two-citizen committee is encouraged to skim unit 2 of *Keep Voting, America* in order to assist the mayor in making further discoveries about the United States of America. But for now, remember the following:

- Good luck.
- Have fun.

- Keep an even keel.
- Be sure to dot your t's and cross your i's. (Ha! Ha!)
- Did I mention that you should have fun?

Notes and dates recorded:

# UNIT TWO

# CHAPTER 10

You are up and running, but first ...

In the late eighteenth century, the Revolutionary War was on. It was brutal and long, but success was ours. We won our independence from England. Finally, the colonists were free to live *without fear of oppression* from the monarch, the king of England. Immediately, the real quandaries came into focus as our Founding Fathers laboriously scripted our federal government into three distinct governing parts. Operating this new nation was to be a simple idea: a check-and-balance system comprised of the law makers, the executive branch, and the court system. You know this from high school civics class—or at least you *did*! The framers of the Constitution and their families were not necessarily whiz kids, nor were they fatuous. The military ranks at the front and the civilians keeping the home front moving smoothly as possible were not wise old men and women, but they were not foolish either. However, at the time, most of the population could not see the vision of these leaders. A few of the many attributes Jefferson and his fellow revolutionaries possessed were tenacity, forward thinking, the ability to compromise, and the vision of freedom for all citizens to pursue their dreams and plans then and now.

We were a free nation administered by a *socially conscious government*. This new country's entire population was free to embrace the right to pursue lives of happiness and prosperity, and in doing so they could avoid falling into the trap of taxation without representation. At least that was the concept. However, freedom wasn't granted to every citizen. Early in our history, women had no voice in government, nor could they own property; black people were hunted down and held as slaves, and they had no vote; American Indians had their lands taken from their tribal members and were displaced and quarantined, and they also had no voting privileges; and children (not old enough to vote) were forced to work alongside full-grown men and deprived of an education. The concept of liberty has always been difficult to wrap one's mind around. Even today people are still struggling to understand what liberty is about.

An unfortunate development in the latter part of the nineteenth century found our new prosperity developing into an expansive divide between the haves and the have-nots. It was between the few who hired and the masses who labored. The number of people setting up shops declined dramatically, and farmers were giving up their plows in droves. The factory was coming of age and beckoning citizens from sea to shining sea and border to border. There was a shift away from the classic American culture, especially agriculture and small shop owners. It was a time of rapid growth. As the Industrial Revolution moved forward, inventors brought to society a multitude of products and the machines to make all those electric toasters. But improvements for each factory worker on the assembly lines would prove to be elusive, resulting in major injuries and sometimes death. All the while, the company owners kept raking in the profits. Dangerous and filthy conditions persisted into the twentieth century. Time-saving devices to lessen the workers' toil were still far off in the future.

To add to this smelly kettle of fish, every time there was a breakthrough in business, other problems popped up. Case in point, the logistics of getting the hordes of products to market became problematic, such as house plans along with all the lumber and nails. However, the gods smiled down on the business owners as more continental railroad tracks were being laid. This ushered in highly efficient marketing tools, transporting new products to an even greater consumer base. The railroads and the goods getting to the home front established a major boon for commerce.

Unfortunately, the act of laying those tracks was riddled with life-threatening danger for the Chinese laborers. The railroad barons chose the demented attitude that the Chinese were disposable. How can so few people cause mayhem for the masses? When the job was done in San Francisco, no technology was around to continue building tracks into the Pacific Ocean so the railroad titans simply turned their backs on their loyal workers. Thus, many did not survive. *This was criminal.* What is outlandish is that there was no punishment in the form of fines or imprisonment levied on the owners of the railroads. The proprietors didn't even get a slap on the wrist for their disreputable neglect of their track layers. It saddens me to know that humans can be so cavalier regarding the health and well-being of the people doing their dirty and extremely dangerous jobs. The Chinese people who survived gathered together in San Francisco and created China Town. Now that is the American way! I'm intensely pleased that such a place has endured and prospered.

The newly invented technologies set the stage for the mass production of a plethora of products. Laborers now had the tools to crank out gluttonous numbers of everything from matches to railway cars. At the same time, industry and land owners stuffed their pockets with the company's profits. Now I'm not opposed to making a profit, but when the employees suffer great hardships (such as serious injury or death, and of course there was no money to pay the doctor or undertaker) just because the big boss wants to hoard all the company's profits, it isn't right! In the olden days before automation, factory owners didn't have the resources for such a score. And then there was automation. This was a *eureka* moment, at least for the industry moguls.

Correspondingly, back-breaking chores in the home could now be done using new inventions like treadle sewing machines to ease a homemaker's misery. The most significant invention was electricity. Soon the homemaker began using devices like the electric iron and the light bulb. Another eureka! People could stay up for hours after dark flooded with light from these new bulbs while happily ironing the breadwinner's work shirt and pants. At inception, this was fabulous! Everyone could enjoy an easier life while listen to the music coming from this new thing called a radio. Everyone?

Unfortunately, the negative aspect of growth reared its ugly head. Because of the increase in revenue, an unusually heightened inclination for greed and deceit surged rampantly throughout the business world. The giant tycoons of industry created an environment that fostered an outrage of contempt escalated by the very people grinding out all those toothpicks: the laborers. As the months and years progressed, it was becoming clear that laborers were paid so little that they couldn't afford the roofs over their heads, much less purchase radios.

Here's something to ponder: if the regular citizens working in the factories could not stretch their wages enough to pay for the products they made, how did the factory owners get so rich? Who was purchasing the company's wares?

The start of the twentieth century brought different kinds of problems to face the US society. American workers were challenging their appalling working conditions in the factories, mining camps, steel mills, garment sweatshops, and agriculture. Tempers flared, and much blood was shed. Distrust and fear ruled the day. Unfortunately, the previous sentence is still true today. Will we ever learn, or are we allowing the almighty dollar to control our every breath, making us blind, deaf, dumb, and even homeless?

The US Constitution came under scrutiny regarding upholding the rights of the labor forces. In many instances, there were no rights. Worker's compensation didn't exist. When the breadwinner of a family died or could no longer maintain his toil in the factory, the family's well-being was in jeopardy.

Fortunately, the nation survived to see a better day, but it did not come right away. In the long run, Prohibition lasted nearly a decade, the debilitating Great Depression another decade, and don't forget the bookends to this story—the two devastating World Wars. Even though all of this happened in the first half of the twentieth century, Americans showed what they were made of: tenacity, courage, strength to carry on, and most of all, love for family and country. Their efforts proved US citizens were steadfast, in part due to an interesting phenomenon called Yankee ingenuity, a slang phrase describing Americans' wherewithal. And they said self-governing wouldn't last.

By the middle of the century, everything had settled down, and lo and behold the American Dream came of age. Gosh, wrap me up in the red, white, and blue. Now people could purchase a home, send their kids to college, buy a boat, open their own businesses, and so on. Enter the middle class—you know, the ones who kept our economy growing? But this only lasted for a couple of generations. Somehow, moral conviction declined, starting with the CEOs of the oilfields and reaching all the way to the gas station attendants. How short is our memory? The lonely gas station attendant's job is rapidly reaching the top of the endangered list of job opportunities. But every once in a while, you can see a proud American still pumping gas and checking the oil. I remember the days when full service was the norm. Do you?

The almighty dollar became a coveted prize toward the end of the twentieth century—worth more than life itself. Greed became unchecked in the form of unlawful bank loans, huge insider trading on Wall Street, and hordes of lobbyists with deep pockets from the big corporations clogging the Senate chamber halls. All the while, the demise of the family continued due to the advertising companies clever buy me ads and the introduction of television as babysitter.

Another bone of contention I have is that the Supreme Court decreed a corporation to be a person. *I beg your pardon!* How infuriating! You will find more information about this appalling notion later in the text. I'm surprised our Founding Fathers haven't resurrected themselves to strike down this ruling.

I started this chapter with the thought of the few controlling the many. Example: The advertising industry is capitalizing on compromise. Beware, consumers—the advertisers are selling you a bill of goods, trying to get you to spend all *your* hard-earned money for *their* products. The advertisers are saying that compromise is not something you should accept when it comes to getting what you want. In part, this is okay if their products are worth the money they are asking. Generally, people compromise all the time—for example, "I will give up my Tuesday bunko game if I'm approved to join your baseball team." That's a reasonable compromise, don't you think? But the dark side of this compromising "game" is when, say, an otherwise congenial woman turns into a "bridezilla," making life miserable for her wedding participants because she flat-out refuses to compromise. Here in America, it's her choice. But I wonder if the bridezilla knows how her behavior comes across to everyone else or just how badly her dealings with friends and family will play out in the future.

My work experience in the garment industry didn't include working in a garment factory commonly known as a "sweat shop". You can image my horror when I came across the story of the tragic Triangle Shirtwaist fire of 1910 in New York City. This is just one gruesome example of how compromised working conditions can escalate into a deadly tragedy. Liberty traverses in every facet of life. America, keep vigilant so we can avoid future catastrophes from the work places with only one exit.

Together with vision, honesty, and follow-through on the part of US Core Citizens, the demise of our liberties can be halted. To start this dialogue, talk about trustworthiness and patriotism during your family council. The more the family knows about the running of our government, the sooner we will improve quality of life for everyone.

I'm going to finish this chapter with my thoughts on a documentary I viewed recently called *Blood on the Mountain*, authored by Chris Hedges. The film is an example of industrial influence on politics, propaganda, greed, confusion, and blatant finger pointing. As I was watching the film, my confusion came from interviews with miners and their families, in which they said various things: (1) one said, "My wife is very sick.... I need this job to buy the costly medicine"; (2) another said, "But we are doing what we want to do"; and (3) they expressed so often the "poor us" mentality and noting things the company wouldn't do for them. Because of the history of tragedies repeated time and again, the miners and their families are not ignorant of the dangers concerning their lives and lungs or the repeated phrase "The laborer can easily be replaced." To paraphrase one of the managements slogans, "You have the obligation to feed your kids. So get back to work." How would you react if your boss said this to you? I, for one, would tell my boss to take this job and shove it!

Greed is on both sides of this coal mining story. On the one hand, the CEO cuts corners and stockpiles profits while on the other hand the worker, hearing about a job in the next county or state, rushes in salivating about the potential cash cow and clambering over the locals trying for the same job. But what worries me the most is when the school is working with the CEO and telling the very young students how wonderful coal mining is for the children, the county, the state, and the country. Coal mining industry is not the only game in town: dairy industry, for one.

The current president is resurrecting the coal mines and at the same time weakening the Environmental Protection Agency. Why can't Americans see past the greed that is ruling us?

Here's a suggestion for the near future. After your council is up and running, encourage each citizen to pick one of the items listed under "More Ideas to Ponder" in chapter 25. It is amazing the truths, real or imaginary, that you will find and how these actions are affecting you and your family's daily lives. In the days before and after your council, each member can research independently and then come together to discuss what they uncovered. This way, the council can explore much more territory. During the research process, you might approach other people about giving a speech at your council. Qualify your speaker; make sure the topic is pertinent and can add to what you already know. In some instances, the speaker can offer a different point of view. This is good training to be openminded.

I'm assuming you are continuing your council plan of going unplugged once a week and talking *with* one another. This program only works if—and this is a big *if*—you want to find out why things work and why things don't work in your home as well as in the local, state, and federal governments. The next thing to do is to vote on the issues.

Notes and dates recorded:

# CHAPTER 11

## Different standards of living

At the beginning of the Industrial Revolution, a lifestyle fueled by greed may not have been the prodigious motivator. However, as the profits gushed in, so did the lust for more money. Several things happened during the late nineteenth century and into the first half of the twentieth century.

1. The US government's hands-off approach to big business gave license to the owners to create monopolies that elevated their standard of living.
2. The promise of a better lifestyle beckoned the families of farmers and small shop owners to work in the factories, paving the way for the ghetto lifestyle.
3. More and more people immigrated from Europe to the United States with visions of a free and prosperous life. After traveling across the pond and stepping into the largest city in America, this new population swelled the number of have-nots into the millions, lowering their standard of living.
4. President Wilson didn't follow through on his word to stay out of the Great War, resulting in a military standard of living.
5. The country went through a decade under Prohibition, the single worst legislation ever to curse the United States, creating an unhealthy standard of living in the form of booze (alcohol, rotgut, hooch, spirits, nasty stuff).
6. If this wasn't harsh enough, the frenzied climate accelerated the country toward an inescapable financial crash in 1929. America was suddenly plunged into deep trouble! The definition for the standard of living at that time became "the soup line." Fortunes were lost and jobs utterly evaporated in the blink of an eye.
7. And then came World War II. There wasn't supposed to be another war after the Great One of 1917. The entertainment industry stepped in and kept the American citizens' morale up as they played their big band sound. Uncle Sam encouraged the GI recruitment to climb. Food and gas rationing, women working in the aircraft factories, jitterbug dance contests, and green stamp collectors all resulted in a mixed bag of lifestyles. It's strange how these adverse events and government programs lowered the standard of living for

the regular citizen and at the same time increased the standards for the mega rich and the federal government. Do you recognize some of these signs today?

Unfortunately, reading about our history doesn't employ any link to current affairs for some citizens or many children in school. As it has through time immemorial, history swaggers on! Because citizens refuse to learn from others' missteps in history, appalling acts against society tend to repeat. Too many parents keep replaying the ugly past, passing their antisocial conduct onto their children instead of working out ways to avoid repeating ill-fated actions. Then the children repeat the dreaded past. It's not fair to saddle current and future heirs with living in the fateful past due to grown-up's short-sightedness.

Things will get better providing we learn from the past and become part of the solution by living in a forward thinking lifestyle!

## Responsible guardians of liberty

Soon after the crash of 1929, "big government" was born. Consuming a decade in our history, the futile attempts to turn our nation around did practically nothing for the man on the street. The powers that be helped only a handful of people, yet hundreds of thousands of US citizens were living below the poverty level. What had been there for the taking was suddenly out of reach. No longer was there a possibility of saving money. Heck, there wasn't enough money to buy a pencil. (Did you know a pencil's graphite can be ground down to be used in different ways? My granddad saved the graphite and used it to clean locks. Everyday folks have been doing things like this for generations. Our ancestors didn't call this recycling; they just did it. Here's a bulletin: recycling did not originate in the twenty-first century!)

As some mystery novels say, it was a dark and stormy night in the nation. Hope for the future vanished for too many people. In the corn and wheat fields, a couple of villains—a devastating drought and the hot dry winds that blew all the topsoil away— caused widespread suffering and a great migration toward the Pacific Coast, human and topsoil both. Nevertheless, during this devastating time, the American citizens, armed with great ingenuity and imagination, developed ways to survive. The unsung heroes saved the day. I do believe that if it hadn't been for American citizens with their Yankee ingenuity, the country would have declined further into despair. The real-life heroes didn't have to slip into those skinny tights and don their masks.

One way of coping with the misery and keeping hunger at bay was gathering together three or four families to share whatever food they had. Another way was hand-sewing rice and flour sacks to use for clothes and window curtains. Regular citizens came together to establish communities throughout the country, making it possible to survive another day. We were holding together, barely. A new lifestyle was slowly emerging: people were on the move, literally.

The New Deal under Franklin D. Roosevelt's administration sponsored several work projects such as artists' painting murals in many post offices and other public buildings, the construction of the Hoover Dam, road works, and most importantly, Social Security (more about this later). Great numbers of people were now working for the government. Still, the suffering persisted until a declaration of war finally stopped the Depression ship dead in the water and sank it. Good riddance to bad rubbish.

Fast forward to the new millennium. The United States was involved in warlike actions in the Middle East but was also supposedly going through a recession. Where did the money come from for all those guns and military advisors? On the flip side, why were so many US citizens stuck living *under* the poverty level while a few couldn't seem to stop spending epic amounts of bucks just so they could own four or five mansions? Something is wrong when huge numbers of our citizens toil inhumanely all day long—that is, if they have jobs. Many families must make basic choices: *Do I get the car fixed or pay the electric bill this month?* This is not American!

Today, the federal government has raised the "big government" baby to the point that the current citizenry is rapidly losing the ability to support their families above the poverty level and is losing the very liberties guaranteed by the Constitution. Here in America, there is plenty of room for all stages of personal finance. Economic growth is the name of the game, not a soggy economy. The greatest damage to our country, in case you haven't noticed, comes in the form of the disappearing essential middle class.

The period of prosperity and excessive spending in America from the mid-1940s to the 1980s (when the middle class really took hold) paved the way to an extremely self-centered lifestyle. That's okay, kind of. Remember, the nation had just come out of a devastating depression and the Second World War. But I find the big spenders' intentions narrow-minded: "We're having such a fine time attending high school football games and towing the Airstream travel trailer to the Grand Canyon that we forgot to keep an eye on our future and the government." Another negative element was the world's disappearing vital resources, like helium, forests, and water.

Now that the baby boomers are heading for Social Security offices across America, we have a huge, newfangled, growing lifestyle developing. Hold on to your paychecks, everybody, because the enormous group of retirees is stepping into the next phase of life, and they want their entitlement. That's a good thing, though, because they earned every penny through their labor. The problem is that there's a new phenomenon materializing in the form of a top-heavy society—the number of retired people will soon outnumber the kith and kin still working for a living. *Heaven help us!*

I want to pause here a moment to address something that irks me to no end. At some obscure time in recent history, the elected officials started dipping their greedy paws into the Social Security funds. These greedy fingers are adversely affecting more people than you can imagine, and I have some questions.

- Where did the money go? The volatile stock markets? Worthless home loans in the 1990s?
- Why are we repeating devastating events?
- Does anyone remember the crash of 1929 when, in part, buying stocks on margin sent the United States into a tailspin, wiping out fortunes and bringing the labor force to its knees?
- Are the wealthy so secure in their independent lifestyles that they don't give a Tinker's Damn about the folks working off their you-know-what for the boss?
- Will future Social Security recipients ever collect their benefits?

In the documentary *PlantPure Nation* concerning Colin Campbell's book *The China Study,* Campbell referenced the struggles he and other experts faced to get government officials to *listen* to facts concerning Americans' poor eating habits and health. I'm borrowing a question from the documentary you might consider adopting. Ask this question on many levels, especially to our government representatives who demonstrate anti-social attitudes: "Why haven't I heard of this?"

Get a grip on your understanding of who is confiscating your paycheck as well as your inalienable rights. I guess I'll let the cat out of the bag. As I write *Keep Voting, America,* my income has been reduced to only what I collect through Social Security. Of course, if I had been more forward thinking earlier in my life and saved money instead of having such a good time, I would be in a better financial situation today. But I'm doing okay thanks to President FDR and his advisors who did some forward thinking and actions during the devastating Depression era. FDR's plan is still standing the test of time, at least for today.

Now back to the uneasy stuff. As if the Social Security Program plight isn't bad enough, the current US debt is astronomical, a terrible financial burden that will spread way beyond the current generation and affect kinfolk not yet born. It is *appalling* how responsible representatives of democracy appear to be lacking in our government.

Overwhelmed? Here's the corker: the general population hasn't a clue what being a responsible guardian of liberty requires of a citizen of the United States of America. Reading the Internet is a start, but I found inspiration in an unlikely place on the side of a Throat Coat organic tea box. It says, "Carefully harvesting limited and sustainable amounts of the bark by hand," they "are maintaining the health of the trees, and preserving this precious resource for generations to come." This is *responsible guardianship!*

I know for a fact that citizens neglect governing our country because I used to be ignorant on such matters. My intention here is not to come across as a recovering whatever but rather to express my newfound sense of responsibility. Through the United States Family Liberty Plan, you can start relearning US history as your family forms its council while slipping into the shoes of US custodians. The purpose is to respectfully guide this great country. And in doing so, we will become patriots ready to advance everlasting freedom. When this happens, we shall all hear the angels singing our National Anthem!

Here's what being a responsible steward of freedom is *not*: denial, tunnel vision, dishonesty, excessive materialism, and offering jobs to experienced workers for minimum pay. Corporate leaders, bank executives, highly paid athletes and entertainers, and public office holders and their families who sit at the top of this food (money) chain must get a grip and assess their extravagant lifestyles for what they are or aren't. First, let's start with denial. Basically, it is a refusal to acknowledge the facts. Denial comes in many different forms. Consider gluttony, which stems from a person's refusal to recognize that he or she can't possibly eat more than his or her stomach can hold. Gluttonous individuals are blindsided by their denial, and they will fight to the death to keep eating. How sad—they just might get there. Denial is mostly counterproductive. As for tunnel vision, you may know it as living in a rut. My father referred to a rut as "a grave with the ends knocked out."

Next, let's look at facts. Facts can be proven, whereas truths can mean different things to different people—and the contradictions never end. Politics, anyone? Let's consider a car crash. All witnesses will have a different version of what led up to the crash depending on where they were prior to the crash. I'm reminded of a movie I watched several times called *Vantage Point*. An enclosed courtyard was the scene of a large gathering of people who were there to hear speeches. Shots were fired, and

STEPHNIE CLARK                                                                46

a bomb exploded. The scene played out several times, with the film rewound from just after the blast back to where each witness entered the scene. Each time the film was played back, you, the viewer could see a different account of what each witness experienced prior to and after the blast. Watching the event repeat throughout the film was a little unsettling at first, but the point was made clear. No two witnesses gave the same report of the event. My conclusion: it makes more sense to gather facts and not rely completely on what people report as "the truth."

Another component in this search for assessing lifestyles is *materialism*. See if you can visualize a cartoon of an overly exaggerated fat man waddling down the street while carrying wads of mostly one-hundred-dollar bills so abundant they keep popping out of every pocket in his expensive suit. Notice that the seams of his jacket and britches are ripping apart. We can all laugh, but then notice the pathetic little people with their tattered clothing scrambling to catch a single bill. There's probably a picture of Washington or Lincoln on the bills—not much value in today's market. Got the image? Now let's turn our attention to the extravagant CEOs, bankers, and entertainment and sports folks and their selfish desires to hold on to all that money.

In the twenty-first century, the federal government and large companies were compelled to create more jobs due to the lingering high unemployment rates across the country. All over America, unemployment rates varied widely. One of the worst-hit areas was Detroit because of its auto industry. No surprise there. But what happened to the technology industry in Silicon Valley? Did anyone see this coming? *Why haven't I heard this before?* The government and the private sector took on this challenge at the request of the president. However, the trickle-down effect reduced dramatically as the money, in the form of wages, filtered down to practically nothing by the time it reached the rank-and-file employees' paychecks. Think *minimum wage*. History appears to be repeating itself, again. Is Congress foolish enough to think that the CEOs of business are helping the economy by offering more jobs in the private sector? Are the CEOs foolish enough to think that Congress is helping the economy by offering more jobs in government? Are we, the wage earners, foolish enough to believe the CEOs and Congress? It's the dreaded us-against-them scenario. *I want to scream!* If a job holder can't even buy an apple for his or her kid, then what's the use of accepting a job for such pathetically low pay?


## A possible formula for employee – employer goodwill relations

A minimum wage *should* be offered to citizen accepting their first job. And once this employee has gained knowledge through education and on-the-job training, their value has increased and so should their pay grade. Employee value and company value have increased. Why are employers replacing experience with youthful energy for the same pay? While the young employee gains the necessary working skills, she or he should work at a lower pay rate. Then, after said skills are proven, heavens to Betsy, the employee should get a raise.

## Responsible guardians of liberty

On the TV show *Shark Tank*, I saw the show airing a man wearing a very long Santa hat who teamed up with one of the "sharks" to further his business of growing and selling live trees at Christmas time. The update is that he hired military vets.

Do you feel as passionate as I do about showing the government our aversion to following a lifestyle of distress, deceit, and unjust taxation? Just as the "sharks" on *Shark Tank* advocated, moneyed people must take the lead and be responsive to not just the vice presidents and shareholders but also to their employees.

I am compelled to remind people that free enterprise *has* a valid place in American society. Every US citizen *has* the right to grow and be prosperous. The government must respond in kind to the regular citizen with suffrage. Question everything and remember, we can vote wayward politicians out of office.

A message to Congress: quit salivating when money people comes a-callin'. And to the wealthy: quit throwing money at Congress just to get legislation handed to you on a silver platter in the form a tax relief. What about the *rest* of the taxpayers' relief?

## A word on paying taxes.

If the 1 percenters start paying their share of taxes *today*, would this amount be equal to, less or greater than the tax collected from the vast citizens of America? Maybe the United States could get closer to being out of debt. A word about the survival techniques and the growing of the tax base during the dark days of the Depression Decade -

But first, I suggest that you talk with senior citizens who lived through the tumultuous 1930s. Ask how they survived the devastating Depression era. Maybe we could adopt some of the survival practices they so apply took upon themselves. You'll be amazed. But you must hurry; this group of citizens is rapidly approaching their centennial years.

I was born in 1939, the last year of the Depression. Even though I didn't experience the debilitating decade firsthand, I was privy to its teachings through my extended family. Americans before, in, and just after my generation grew up solving our individual problems with the guidance of our parents, who taught us to live moral and virtuous lives and pay our taxes. This influence helped each generation understand the value of how the tax money was helping us live a healthy and harmonious life. However, things changed during the second half of the century. Too many children did not receive the benefit of the treasured family teachings and do not have the sensitivity to realize how the tax dollar helps our society to be prosperous. How pathetic is that? (To express sensitivity does not mean that you are frail and easily hurt. Instead, sensitivity can mean having compassion for others.)

A major change in the attitudes of Americans happened almost overnight. Just because *you* didn't think of something, why do you toss out everything that came before you? A case in point is the young house hunters' badmouthing the old, *outdated* interior designs, equipment, music, and so on. Too many citizens today are unknowing and uncaring, dismissing it all. I really don't get this one. What the American family has lost is steadfastness of character, the ability to identify society's purpose and recognizing how tax dollars keep American's progressing forward as we journey through life.

## Present-day worries

Today, Americans are being tested again, only this time the betrayal is coming from every conceivable segment of our daily lives:

- pharmaceutical laboratories
- political appointees
- business monopolies
- federally funded bankers conducting business for their own selfish desires as they did in the late nineteenth century
- threats coming from other parts of the globe
- rogue law enforcement officials here at home
- overpaid sports players and entertainment figures (the newest members of this assemblage)

The perfidy toward voting citizens, employees, and small bank depositors is crippling the country. During the 1980s, I had a savings account at what I thought was a reputable and well-established bank. Wouldn't you know—one day I stepped into the bank, had to stand in a line reminiscent of a meandering river for nearly thirty minutes just so I could withdraw some money, and guess what? The bank executives had set into motion a fee system that ate up *all* my money! Since then I have maintained money accounts in a credit union. Once burned, twice shy!

But let's get back to politics. I'm reminded of a woman credited with spearheading the anarchist movement in North America. A passage from E. L. Doctorow's book *Ragtime* comes to mind:

> A man stood and shouted. Goldman held up her hands for quiet. "Comrades, let us disagree, of course, but not by losing our decorum to the extent that the police may have an excuse to interrupt us." People turning in their seats indeed saw now a dozen policemen in the crowd at the door.

Today, countless people either do not fully understand how the Great Depression transpired or elect not to accept what happened. Regrettably, the unchecked greed dating from the Industrial Revolution has been revived and is once again a runaway train on its way to a wreck in the twenty-first century. Talk about dishonesty! Do not kid yourselves. The veil of despair is here again!

There is a new wrinkle to our story that adds to the mayhem of the greedy bunch. I didn't say Brady Bunch, although the entertainment and news industries are constantly reminding us of how muddled life has become. (Here's a quick English lesson: *constant* means "never ending," while *continual* means "very frequent." Celebrities are *constantly* joining the 1 percenters in terms of dollar amount only. Celebrities *continually* say, "Look at me and how rich I have become." Their reckless and thoughtless spending drives the price of any- and everything out of reach for the other 99 percent. Purchasing a three-hundred-thousand-dollar car is excessive, but then if you have such an abundant amount of cash, why not? But, take a moment to think of how this purchase affects the prices of all automobiles. And while we are on this subject, why not take that money to help refurbish a rundown park? You might become a genuine American hero! Nice, but don't let this new fame go to your head. There's too much work we need to finish.)

I must admit there is a crusade of sorts afloat. First-generation families, who have amassed wealth recently, are joining the ranks of the philanthropic society. If these movers and shakers, the new members of the employers group, would pay a decent wage to the people who work for them, we wouldn't have the ever-growing need for charity. This is my take on stewards of the land!

Let's take a moment for a word of encouragement. I'm here to tell you there *is* life among the voting citizens. In 2011, the senior citizens residing in my town successfully collected enough signatures required for a referendum. We had a lawyer craft the proper wording for the referendum, and then it was up to my fellow senior citizens and me to collect over 15,000 signatures, although we needed only 7,600 to ensure that our issue would be put on the voting ballot. To see our referendum published on the ballot on Election Day 2012 was an extremely happy adrenaline rush. And then the votes came in. To read our account of that year, turn to A11 in the appendix.

To those who do not understand the past, I say, *don't inhabit the past*. Instead, gain knowledge from it.

Notes and dates entered:

# CHAPTER 12

The United States Core Citizen family's struggles continue to grow.

Let's identify the three types of American family units:

1. The family that strives to enjoy a high standard of living with all its toys
2. The family eking out a subsistence living
3. The family living off of government handouts

I left out the entire middle segment of American families from this list. This larger part of our population essentially supported the American economy—that is, until recently. For all intents and purposes, Middle America has nearly vanished. Several events have caused this demise: our runaway Congress raising the debt ceiling in tandem with Congress and the Supreme Court showing favoritism toward the large corporations and mega banks by creating loopholes for the rich and ignoring the citizens; corporations' sending jobs overseas, creating devastatingly high unemployment; state and local governments spending millions of promissory notes on programs that we, the people, do not want; and lobbyists encouraging Congress to amend our Constitution beyond recognition. Wait a minute, let's back up a bit. What's this about "promissory notes"? Who gave the government permission to hurl the country into massive debt? The money from the pathetically low-paying jobs, generated by government and corporations, isn't enough to replace the threadbare clothes of American families. Middle Americans, meet the poverty group!

As I write *Keep Voting, America,* the executive branch of our government surprised the American people with the Affordable Health Care Act (AHCA). Sadly, the president encumbered the American population with impossible deadlines to "get health insurance" and then levied monstrous fines when citizens did not comply. My Social Security check was reduced by $105 a month. Well, there goes the budget for my Curves visits, which have kept me in good health for several years. And I'm not the only one. Several major problems occurred; large numbers of citizens lost what health coverage they already had. And because many did not choose a health-coverage group by the designated time (maybe there was too much confusion hindering their decision process), they are now saddled with penalties that will probably follow them to the grave. *All these legislative decisions are not working.* The United States is drowning in debt. *Where is our lifeline?*

As if this weren't incapacitating enough, the most damaging risk to liberty comes in the form of individuals and families from all walks of society becoming *complacent* regarding how the country is run. Everybody wants to talk about their own agenda, cutting out all others and professing the country's ailments are the other guy's fault. Geez, Louise! There's too much partying going on, and for what? This doesn't feel right. Too many people are taking the attitude that money is for burning and to heck with the future. What we are witnessing is greed in the form of "I want it my way—forget the compromising—and I want it *now!*" Your free lunch counter is closed.

## Things that are up-to-date today may be rejected tomorrow

Have you watched the HGTV shows on which American citizens in their early adult years, ages twenty to thirty, are wildly searching for their "perfect" homes even if they are way beyond their already unrealistic budgets? They walk the walk and talk the talk, but do they fully understand how the walk and talk work? Remind me—what's a budget for? What they want today will be ghastly outdated before they know it. The young people's likely future will include a growing disillusionment of their "perfect house." Hopefully their income will stay abreast of their expenses, allowing the new property owners to make the needed *updates* in a month or so without much suffering to their bank account.

Why are young folks so quick to criticize what has gone on before them? Thumbing their nose at what is perceived as outdated shows their lack of understanding of where things came from. If it's not broken, don't fix it. If it wasn't for the research and development process of ideas and products in the seventeenth through the twentieth centuries, we wouldn't have television, the polio vaccine, indoor plumbing, and yes, continuing freedoms.

Back to the perfect house: compromise is no longer an option for young house hunters. What irritates me the most is their self-important attitude sending them into despair if they don't get all that stuff: PDQ! (If you don't know what *PDQ* means, check out appendix A8.) Remember my earlier reference to bridezilla. I only hope they learn from their failures and recover enough to not repeat the same blunders. A mother can dream! In the meantime, be smart about making large financial decisions, okay?

The devastatingly naïve decisions that ill-informed people make affects the whole economy deleteriously. Think of it this way: the stone pitched into the pond creates waves that reverberate in every direction. Here's a fun activity you can do as a family: skip stones across the surface of a lake. Take your time to practice several times so you can gain your bragging rights. But once you get it, what fun you will have with your family. How many times can you get one stone to skip across the surface of the pond? At my recent weight-loss at Curves, we were asked what we could do outside in the sunshine. I suggested the rock skipping and added the benefit of sharring the fun with family and friends.

Human nature tells us we need to experience an occasional failure in order to succeed in life. It is easier to recover when the failure is not a three-quarters-of-a-million-dollar house that will be outdated next week. I hope these movers and shakers wake up and see the future trepidations they are instigating. And another thing, hefty monthly mortgage payments are enough to choke a water buffalo. People with excessive greed, as I have mentioned several times in this book, cast a wide net, negatively affecting thousands of people they've never met. Don't burden yourselves with instant bad debt like our politicians have been doing for decades—consider our trillion-dollar liability as an example. Hells bells, who told the Congress they could get away with such highway robbery? Talk about unrealistic and that all popular phrase: "That's not my job, ma'am!"

Here's a possible way you can curtail wasteful spending. During family council, citizens with and without suffrage sort out a trustworthy program for handling money and other resources. Some suggestions are as follows:

- You might ask a bookkeeper to give a talk at one of your councils about compounding penalties. What a nightmare—the penalties, not the bookkeeper.
- Follow the money needed to run your city; you will find some eye-opening figures. But don't be alarmed at such large dollar amounts. Remember, this is a *city* budget you're researching.
- Follow the campaign money trail. This is reasonably easy to do on the Internet!
- You might scrutinize reasonable expenditures—you know, the ones that have a much better likelihood of producing down-to-earth outcomes without thrusting your council into endless debt. Discuss your findings at council. I could go on and on, but you get my drift.

Another useful activity for the family council is to gain a better understanding of what the American society is *truly* about from the ground up by referencing a book on etiquette. Keep an open mind, please. Your reading will bring you up to speed on the ethical lifestyles parents and grandparents passed down to their children ever since, well, before the "white folk" stepped foot on this land. Also, *Reminisce* magazine is an excellent resource for down-to-earth stories of how families coped through trying times. Better yet, read the magazine with senior members of your family. I'll bet your grandparent or a senior neighbor is longing to share some personal stories about how they managed to live in harmony and peace against all odds way back then. Hearing stories about your family's past beats the heck out of watching TV shows like Housewives of Whatever City. I do hope the TV shows' depiction of a lifestyle hasn't become the norm!

## Empty manners

Nearing the end of the twentieth century, the teachings of manners and respect turned up in the public-school rooms, making these strengths meaningless and unwanted. Another invasion of our minds is that television programming appears to be destroying the family teachings of social and moral skills as the executives promote shows like *Here Comes Honey Boo Boo* and hateful programs such as the overabundant reality talk shows. Honestly, these shows are shouting matches where nothing is accomplished. With the advent of cell phones bringing these televised shows upfront and close (she sighs), there is no place for a person to escape. I feel like we are being inundated with anti-American propaganda.

I came up with a whole list of books on manners other than authors like the Amy Vanderbilt's and Emily Posts. Your understanding of the different cultures might be helped by reading the different mindsets on the topic of etiquette.

- *Masonic Etiquette Today*
- *Etiquette for Chauffeurs*
- *Russian Etiquette and Ethics in Business*
- *Cookies: Bite Size Life Lessons*
- *Etiquette with the Quran*
- *The English Gentleman*
- *Heading Out on Your Own*
- *A Pug's Guide to Etiquette*
- *Dude, That's Rude!*
- *Etiquette for Dummies*
- *Miss Manners*
- *I Try to Behave Myself*
- *The American Flag: A Handbook of*
- *Prison Etiquette*
- *Golf Etiquette*
- *Etiquette for Young Moderns*

The list is just the tip of the etiquette book mountain.

Some people think manners have dissolved into oblivion. I hope not! Wherever the social skills have faded to, we must come to terms with the situation and get them back. Science teaches us that things don't disappear or evaporate; they merely change form. I don't like the form that has been rising out of the obliteration of politeness and courtesy. What say you?

Another place where the loss of social skills is escalating is retail stores. Are the employees unhappy with their jobs? What do they know that the boss doesn't want the shoppers to know? No wonder people are making their purchases through the Internet. Speaking of the Internet, I read an article on Time.com titled "19 Words That Will Make People Like You More." My favorite: "I'll find out." This phrase signals that you are taking the "proactive approach," offering helpful assistance and going out of your way to do so. See? There is hope!

Diametrically opposite is the most bureaucratic phrase known to humankind, uttered incessantly by some of the least likable people: "That's not my job!" A more current phrase: "That's above my pay scale." If we could just get past the, one up–one down syndrome and talk in terms of two steps forward and, maybe, on occasion, half a step back, we just might see some progress toward a more rewarding and pleasant life. Whatever floats your boat in terms of a happy and prosperous life has got to be better than ravaging the country and turning it into a dust bowl.

**Rule Seven:** No finger pointing; no whining.

Here's another fun suggestion. At Family Political Councils, when the "wind in your council sails" stops due to finger pointing, feel free to borrow the sign idea from the boxing arena. Have a citizen walk around the room holding up a sign. (Keep your business clothes on—no bikinis.) On the sign is a circle, and inside the circle is a drawing of a hand pointing. A diagonal line is drawn across the hand. Hopefully everyone will see the humor and keep paddling until the wind once again fills the sails. Then the council can resume the journey with happiness.

## More manners

Good manners must preside as the highest priority, especially when very young children are present. Our nation's official documents safeguard every US citizen's right to establish goals toward a morally virtuous life. You can't have one of the following without including all:

- liberty
- justice
- domestic tranquility
- common defense (this is where the feds can come in handy provided they do not overstep their boundaries)
- the pursuit of a happy life

The following excerpt is taken from *Our Country's Founders*, edited with comments by William J. Bennett.

> Where moral purity can be impossible, the practice of good manners is not. And who knows, the more we practice, the better we may actually become.

## A description of the traditional/modern American family

The common family unit in the United States is composed of a mother, a father, and 2.4 (or 2.6) children. But there are many other combinations making up American families.

a)  the couple, married or not, without children
b)  the mother or father is missing
c)  both parents are missing; grandparent(s) step in to keep the children together
d)  a child still under the age of eighteen raising his or her younger siblings
e)  the foster home
f)  mom in prison but the kids visit often
g)  grandparent living with the family

The list goes on and on. Any one of these families has the potential to go unplugged and talk *with* one another. We need to build a future made up of active voters if we are going to guarantee the continuation of liberty. Or if the family members are at odds with one another and like it that way, they could remain on a collision course toward estrangement. The choice is up to each United States Core Citizen: the family. At-risk families, going through the process in this book could help reduce the statistics concerning overcrowded jails. Letter f above, moms in prison, is one group I would like to encourage the building of their Family Political Councils. Think about it—they meet once a week or so at the same time in the same place. This could work!

If the family is small, with two people or so, think about filling in the vacant political offices with people you get along with and invite them to visit your council. Coworkers and neighbors can see for themselves your family's potential to communicate with high standards even though members may not reflect others' points of view. All participants bring with them different approaches to getting things done. This is politics! Please, leave your foul words and attitudes somewhere else; they have no place in council. If you pursue less-than-socially-conscious communication and resort to shouting, uplifting joy falls to the floor and dies a miserable death. That is not what we want.

## Dictatorship, benevolent dictatorship, or family political council

Throughout history, the nuclear family unit has demonstrated a form of *dictatorship,* where the children (even adult children) and their mother, sometimes even a grandparent, are subjects of the father. Only the father dictates what happens within the family concerning financing, planning vacations, discipline, and so on. The dictator does not do chores like cleaning the dishes, taking out the trash, making the beds—you know, the mundane stuff. For some families, it's up to the mom and the kids to hold secrets from the head of household. This builds distrust for authority characters, but how will the transition from the family home to the greater society play out? Today, the wretched dark side of oppressed families appears to be taking over on a grand scale:

- Too often an ostensibly healthy family falls apart.
- The head of household rules by force, and the hold on the family could escalate toward exerting physical and mental harm.

In my assessment, living in a dysfunctional environment conjures up a pathetic lifestyle. Discouraging citizens of the family from seeking a happy and profitable existence must not occur. The head of household's iron-fisted control does not have to be the model for the US Core Citizen, the family. Far from it!

## Citizen domination

Currently, the US government is taking over the very lives of many voting citizens. I see countless US residents who are at a loss, not knowing what to do about their vanishing liberties. Still more citizens are completely clueless. In several states, the right to vote is deviously manipulated to keep many citizens *from* the voting booth. This is wrong!

Wake up American citizens. Big government and big money (corporations as well as big banks), collectively and in secret, are whittling a pathway to government domination as they cut down every tree in the Northwest. *Please* don't let them annihilate the redwood forest in Northern California. Last year I took a trip to visit Humboldt College, whose campus looks like it is growing right out of the redwood forest. What a magnificent and almost biblical experience it was walking through the trees. As I emerged from the forest, I kept thinking, *There is room for all US citizens to enjoy all of the country's national treasures.* Excuse my wonderings, but every American has the right to go about their lives without *fearing* total government power. Having the freedom to roam our national treasures like the ageless redwood forest must *never end.* The 1 percenters need to rethink what they are doing to our forests. Walk away from whatever is ailing you and smell the redwoods. This is what I enjoy! Your nervous system will thank you for your forward thinking and actions.

Here's something to ponder. Tax revenues are supposed to support our government programs—no surprise there. And yet, federal, state, and local government programs are at the risk of imploding. Maybe it's because the sheer number of government programs is careening out of control. Taking tax revenue away from worthy social programs is part of the problem. A chilling thought just went through me: *What would happen if the following government programs were halted or limited?*

- elder-care programs such as Meals on Wheels
- protection of our clean drinking water
- education for our children (Poor things, they cannot vote. Hopefully, their parents do!)
- state and national parks, big and small

Do you really want the government to collapse? Things are looking good for the citizens of this country, kind of. On our present course, programs like affordable housing won't last much longer. The US society as we know it may not exist beyond the midway point of the twenty-first century. Come on, Americans, don't let this happen. As you can see, I get a little rowdy when natural habitats are adversely affected and the American lifestyle is threatened.

Notes and dates recorded:

# CHAPTER 13

Resuming a nation of wealth and social order is possible!

The world looks to the United States as a nation of wealth: streets lined with gold, billionaires on every corner, an attorney in every man's pocket, citizens owning multiple businesses, closets as big as a four-bedroom house, and corporations exempt from paying taxes. Wait a minute—unfortunately, the last one does exist! But are the other five realistic? No! When immigrants come to America, do they have stars in their eyes, expecting to have instant wealth, a luxury car or three, a thirty-thousand-square-foot house, multiple swimming pools with waterfalls, loads of toys and electronic stuff, ruby and diamond rings on every finger and even on toes, and maybe a helicopter? (There is no denying I have a vivid imagination.) The people who own this stuff are part of the 1 percent of the US population and generally thought of as "old money." The newbies to this elite club, professional sports people and entertainers, have the money but not much power or sense of dignity. And then there are the 99 percenters who are struggling to pay rent, which is keeping them from ever owning so much as a tiny abode complete with one infinitesimal bathroom and a closet a foot and a half wide! But what the working stiffs and I possess is Yankee ingenuity, paving the way to figure things out! A few years back, I rented an old-time cottage in Washington State. Me, my sewing machine and I fixed it up real nice. It's good to have lots of skills to draw from.

So where do you fall in the US population? Americans are known to profit from financial security along with all the stuff I mentioned above and much more. Are you interested in all that greed? The attraction for what mega money can fetch blindsides folks and turns them away from the reasons that people of the world traveled to America:

- freedom from oppression
- freedom to worship as they wish
- freedom to move about the country without having to carry a passport
- freedom to speak out against government corruption and not be killed for their effort
- freedom to run our country
- freedom to strive for and realize each citizen's dream
- freedom to pursue an education

These ideals have motivated US citizens for more than two hundred and fifty years and have inspired us to protect and follow the Constitution. Not many countries on the globe can guarantee these liberties for all its citizens. All people living in the United States, and this includes immigrants as well, must relearn the purpose of *liberty everlasting!* The important goal is to keep an open mind and communicating with one another in your Family Political Council. Excessive greed is no way of life. As the old saying goes, "You cannot take it with you!"

## Social order

Believe it or not, we have an established social order right here in the good ol' US of A. Citizens in this social order have survived and, more importantly, have blossomed for eons. Unfortunately, those who chose to ignore social order have become the poster children for the American population.

We need to show our patriotic side by rekindling our Founding Fathers' zeal and revitalize our precious liberties. Too many citizens have abused freedom for the past fifty or so years. Do we have to work at patriotism? Yes, just like we must work at maintaining our social order as well as our bridges and highways. As citizens, we must prove our courage and extend our gratefulness for inheriting the Declaration of Independence. Reclaiming our vanishing liberties for the future is doable. It is prudent that we act now!

Not tomorrow. Not next year. Now!

We are a country of many different lifestyles. A dialogue on the various historical social behaviors could bring about a better understanding of why they exist. I'll start the dialogue with, "Women are fully capable of opening their own doors." Too many times, I was almost knocked down when a man took it upon himself to rush past me just to open the door. In doing so, he would get in my way, causing me to become a contortionist just so I could enter the building. With the advent of electricity, opening the door has made a man's chivalrous gesture obsolete. Oh, well! Old-fashioned social gestures are nice, but let's examine them a little more closely. I really don't want a box of chocolates; just hanging out together is good for me.

Notes and dates recorded:

# CHAPTER 14

## A happy and productive society

*Procrastination isn't happening; therefore, keep dreaming as you take charge!*

Developing your Family Political Council will potentially uncover benefits while follow the plan described in chapters 4 through 8. Start your journey toward a well-informed and more productive life in what has been known for several centuries as a fine place to live in a well-thought-out society from shore to shore and border to border: the United States of America. But these facts are incomplete. As you know, last century a couple of spots located on the globe not physically touching the continental United States chose to join the Union—a sincere Alaskan welcome in the Yupik language, *Wagaa!* pronounced "wah-kaw," and a kindhearted Hawaiian welcome in the island language, *Aloha!*

By and large, we are a nation of dreamers and achievers. That's why American citizens stand tall. Some dreamers achieve great heights like building safe and pleasing environments in order to have a happy, uplifting society of people—for example, architect Frank Lloyd Wright. Many people continually work to build better mousetraps, so to speak—for example, Thomas Edison and his crew. During the past two hundred years, the citizens living in our urban and metropolitan civilizations have nudged the essence of liberty across all lines of society. Folks in the eighteenth century respected this new idea of liberty and kept on dreaming.

## Education and dreams

But not all Americans were born with the dream gene. Americans validate every day their ability to generate enough passion to help those who are not able to dream. The name of some relatively recent legislation comes to mind: No Child Left Behind. We should aim to leave no child behind regardless of whether they are male or female or what the color of their skin is, their religion, their economic situation, or their IQ. This proclamation encouraged Americans to make sure that children are offered a chance at living a *decent* and *trusting* existence through education, giving them the tools with which to make dreams come true. Many citizens of countries around the globe are denied education, preventing any dreams from ever forming.

Think of the materials in print and on film that you can find on the public library shelves. How would you like it if books, television, the Internet, and libraries were no longer available? To enhance the print and film availability, the American classroom offers students young and old a platform, and hopefully a safe environment as well, assisting all of us in fulfilling our dreams. In theory, this sounds great. But we still need more reinforcement through our extended families and close friends in order to advance the prospect of undertaking a well-mannered and responsible life for all citizens. The most important and basic education comes from parents' and extended families treasured social teachings.

Here's a brief look at my second effort to get a college education. In my 50s I returned to college and found I still had dreams and the courage to make them come true. University of Hawaii, what a fabulous experience. I took all sorts of history classes. Asian art, theater, Religions of the world, US history. When we got to the 1940s, I laid my pen down and reminisce with all my teacher. I would look around the lecture hall realizing my fellow students were still etching out notes. Religions of the world—Wow! I had no idea there were so many. Theater, never in my wildest dreams did I think I would be in the audience watching a Kabuki play, but there we were. My twelve-year old son and I were captivated by the display of Japanese theater. After five semesters I transferred to the North-West and attended Shoreline Community College where I found myself on the dean's list, my first time. Here's where one of my designs became a reality: the golfer's ash-tray. Well, not my greatest accomplishment. But that is a whole other story, someday I'll tell you about it. A decade later I enrolled in South Puget Sound Community College. This was the most rewarding period of my educational experience. Again, I'm an honor student, but it's what I did with my education that matters. Vice President of Alpha Xi Phi chapter, parade float committee chair, fund raiser for Habitat for Humanity and drafts person for four families through Habitat for Humanity. I didn't save the world, but I made many people happy. I could go on about a good education, but I think you can see the value when a person puts in the effort in the right envirnment.

Here's another suggestion for you. Mozilla is asking citizens to get behind the effort to save the Internet's net neutrality. The folks at Firefox offer a compelling argument to keep the world's Internet free from government domination and special interests group. I encourage everyone to read about their efforts.

## When it comes to opportunity and the responsibility that comes with it...

What the voting public does with any opportunity is purely up to every individual. Democracy tells us there is no excuse to inflict adverse suffering on people's dreams. Never forget that we all live in a free society; therefore, please don't rain on anyone's parade just because they are different. I have used several key words and phrases to describe liberty. Can you add to this list?

- informed
- following dreams
- achieving opportunities (keep them legal)
- standing tall
- happy and uplifting
- "no child left behind"
- decent and trustworthy
- well-mannered and responsible
- passing on treasured family social teachings to each generation
- free to vote

If you need more reading to activate your dreams for the future, I encourage you to get a copy of the late Robin Williams's book *Everybody's Got Something*. He left us a handsome legacy of pure humor. Williams will live in our funny bones forever. Another public person who left a legacy is Shirley Temple. During the darkest hours of America's history, she sang and danced in many films, one being *The Little Colonel*. Temple earned a special place in the hearts of many generations of Americans, forever.

Our lives are made better because of the willingness of dreamers (like Williams) to follow their visions. Americans have offered hundreds of millions of innovations to a widespread public in the past two hundred years. Social Security tax (FICA), paved roads, heart transplants, and the assembly line are some of the many innovations that we now rely upon as we go through our daily lives. A few mighty wonderful improvements have come from American dreamers:

- extending daylight through electricity
- prolonging a healthy life through good nutrition
- providing much-needed comic relief

These and many more benefits make life worthwhile whether you are a wage earner struggling to pay the bills, part of the management team making great efforts to keep the production line going, or the CEO offering the jobs. However, keep in mind where we came from and how we evolved, living in a country where liberty abounds and trumps all other forms of government. I hope you noticed the absence of the word *wealthy*. Heavens to Betsy—America's streets are *not* paved with gold. Far from it, what with all the potholes in the pavement, deep cracks in the bridges, as well as the crumbling water and sewage pipes.

The high standard of living we have developed *demands* a maintenance program in order to keep the aging infrastructure in good operating condition. Who knew? Housewives did!

## Happiness, prosperity, growth, maintenance

When repair schedules fall through the cracks (pun intended), leaving said cracks exposed to decay, the taxpayers are the ones who pay dearly in the form of fees and penalties, making the bottom line—gee, there doesn't seem to be a bottom line. As the problems continue to grow, threatening our everyday lives, the dollars add up fast. This growth isn't a good thing! The real damage is done when chaos becomes the norm due to the miles of red tape generated by politicians and lawyers. Recently, the politicians in my town cut jobs in the highway and sewage system maintenance departments. Not good planning! Politicians are calling these reductions in force (RIF) *budget cuts.* How on earth can they sleep at night when they say this is an acceptable way of operating our city? What a big mess it will be when our aging sewage pipes burst—and what a cost to the public at large. Heck, forget the cost; it's threatening our health and safety. In 2016, the University of California–Los Angeles, Kearny Mesa (a community in San Diego), and Orange County experienced tons of water flowing everywhere except through the pipes. Millions of gallons of water washed away due to the pipes' bursting. And the entire state of California is in an extreme drought! This is truly bad. No, this is ruinous. I don't know about the rest of the country, but Southern California is reeling from neglect. Maybe we can persuade the politicians to roll up their sleeves, pick up a shovel, and help clean up this mess. Why are people free to be creative and dream of a better life but are not cognizant of maintenance programs? I know I don't dream about catastrophes costing all of us taxpayers money we don't have.

**Rule Eight:** All citizens are to dress appropriately and be on time for all councils!

Notes and dates recorded:

# CHAPTER 15

Topics worth talking about—remember, this is politics!

- Our elected political representatives have been passing questionable laws for decades. How have they done that?
- Are some existing laws so convoluted that they cannot be carried out?
- What is missing in these laws?
- Has the public become so intolerant of others and then demanded that Congress make more and more laws to deal with "undesirable" people?
- How did US corporations and the federal government get so powerful?
- Why are we, the voting citizens, letting the US Congress, the individual states, and city councils pass these unwanted laws? (One thought is that citizens are being fed *misinformation*.)
- Can the citizens with suffrage stop the ruination of our Constitution? Yes! But how?
- Do you really know *why* our Constitution was written?
- In the beginning, we did not have corporations. Insatiable greed has made US corporations a menace to a respectful society. And what's up with corporations being legally considered people? Not only do I not get this, *I don't want this!*
- Who benefits under the current social order? Who does not? US vets? Low-paid individuals as well as their families? Job injury victims? Legal immigrants? Mega millionaires? Politicians? A variety of ethnic groups?
- What if the voting citizens wrote a new constitution? (*wink, wink*)
- Why were the unpopular speeches, letters, and publications from the oppressed citizens left out of our history books? After all, they are a huge part of our history. The good and the bad, the right and the left, progressive and conservative, popular and unpopular, memorable and vague—what about the middle ground? You know, the gray area? There is a lot of room here for talking politics.
- How about condensing the text on wars? Instead, expand the positive human element. *We need to know more about how this country has nurtured its citizens!*
- It's unfortunate that the Prohibition law was passed, as it became the most unwanted law of the land. What about the Equal Rights Amendment? Why did it fail?

- Could money be talking too loudly, rendering most citizens unable to think clearly?

I told you there is a host of ideas to talk about and projects to build. At this point, keep it steady as you go, and take only one tack at a time. When following these actions, Americans will become clear thinkers! NICE!

Notes and dates recorded:

# Chapter 16

Pick any of the following nineteen goals. Your project can be done quickly, or you may opt to take several months to complete it. Have fun!

**Rule Nine:** Don't give up your powers by doing nothing!

Goal One: Encourage all citizens.

Regardless of whatever disability a family citizen might have, I implore you to include him or her as part of your active council. For example, I have a learning disability. Most of my life, people discouraged me from dreaming, and heaven forbid I should pursue those dreams. Don't protect family members from *trying*. We have too much work ahead of us to exclude anyone. In order to reach your goals along the way to success, you must fail from time to time. Here's my advice: pick yourself up, dust yourself off, and start from where you left off. This way, you can learn from your *missteps*.

At the ripe old age of sixty-five, I started writing. To date, I am a published author with three more works nearing the finish line. (Better late than never, as the saying goes!) Unfortunately, failure for many people is impossible to bear. But disappointments shouldn't hold anyone back. In fact, it fans the flame to fruition. (Say that five times fast.) Remember, the ability to dream and to make dreams come true is as American as hot dogs and Mom's apple pie. You will be amazed to find out just how much the physically and mentally challenged citizens are itching to bring to the table:

- energy to get the job done
- humor just to lighten things up a bit
- an innate understanding of how things work
- a couple hundred ideas of things to do
- courage to follow through
- a cornucopia of skills to be tapped

Be sure to use some form of decorum to keep your Family Political Council productive and not fall into a hysterical free-for-all as seen on some reality television shows. Remember, the next president of the United States of America is a vital member of an American family.

As a side note, I want to introduce you to a short film that aired on CBS. It is about Kermit's letter regarding his early life as a tadpole. In countries around the globe where dictators or terrorists suppress the people, his message would never see the light of day. I do hope you get a chance to watch the film; it is worth viewing again and again. Well done, Kermie!

Goal Two: Write a letter to the newspaper editor or your state legislator.

It is common knowledge that the technology industry is outpacing the law and creating many avenues for socially inept people to prey on unsuspecting, law-abiding citizens. The technology involved is the throwaway cell phones. In fact, one day I received a phone call—I won't go into detail here, but the gist of the call was that the caller, my "grandson," wanted me to wire him a fairly large sum of cash so he could get home.

After the caller hung up on me, I called the telephone company, but they could not do anything to help me find out where the call had come from. Hence the throwaway phone! I then called the police and learned that the fraud department couldn't do anything unless I sent the money. Fat chance! As it turns out, my grandson was not where the caller (impersonating my grandson on the phone) said he was. Causing people, especially strangers, inexcusable worry about something that isn't real is *not nice!* When a voice on the other end of the phone gives you the impression that something is terribly wrong, it just might be a scam.

If you are targeted with this or any other scam, play along with the caller. He or she will eventually hang up. Eureka! You just foiled their game. It's nice that the joke is on the lowlife who wasted his or her time by dialing your number.

Now for some politics. Law-abiding citizens can do several things to persuade our legislators to bring the law up to speed with the out-of-control technology industry. You might send a *handwritten* letter to the state as well as federal lawmakers. Send a message of your malcontent to the local newspaper in the form of a letter to the editor. Keep the tone of your message polite while making your point. Maintain a dialogue with everyone you know. Get creative because the baddies are crafty. For your council, this action is perfect for a subcommittee to get their teeth into.

> **Rule ten:** All family citizens are to associate freely and must be included in nearly all aspects of your council.

Goal Three: Walking the walk, or crewing your ship (council)

In a safe environment, each family citizen can display the ability to work toward a peaceful but spirited, in a good way, wholesome and uplifting lifestyle within the home and into the greater society of America. This harmonious lifestyle will fill up your every day. There will be very little, if any, time to—shall we say—go off the rails and mess up your life. Excepting the occasional human frailty, the aim is to move forward into a life of harmony and prosperity.

In the beginning, guide the family toward a benevolent dictatorship. The word *benevolent* softens the edges of *dictatorship* and keeps the family more or less balanced and in check. In order for this to happen, all family members are invited to participate. But let's take a step forward: replace the benevolent dictatorship with the United States Family Liberty Plan. *All* family citizens, even children without suffrage, have a say in your council. We can change an old-fashioned model from a despot family unit toward a modern governed-by-the-consent-of-the-governed political family unit. I wonder if this is how our ancestors lived their family lives. In their full capacity, the Family Political Council can bring to the table a desire to foster a clean and healthy, even happy, crew as you sail your council ship toward governing the United States. As your family grows into adulthood, council influence can have a positive, far-reaching impact on the greater society. But I must be cautious while encouraging this kind of activity. It saddens me to think that some American families could develop this plan against humanity. Lord knows we see enough of this through newscasts coming from the hot spots around the globe.

I sincerely hope that each family follows the plan with regard to socially accepted behaviors *instead* of testing how far each council member can stay ahead of the laws of the land.

Just a note: Be sure to have the egg timer or a stopwatch going while citizens give their orations; this way no one will be scolded for taking away another citizen's time at the podium.

Goal Four: The aim is to allow children to participate in council while maintaining decorum. A word of caution: it is better to use low levels of encouragement when inspiring your children to talk in council.

*The Special Kid:* An idiom comes to mind: "Give them an inch, and they'll take a mile." For several years, parents have been telling their kids how *special* they are. Raising the bar too high by praising children's actions and words gives the kids a false sense of themselves. Let's stay away from telling children they are special because, if everyone is special, then *special* loses its true luster and turns out to be ordinary. We can't all be special; it just doesn't work that way. Have I worn out the word *special* yet? If a job is well done, then say in a matter-of-fact-voice, "Well done" or "Good job!" If the kid's venture falls short or has lost its momentum, work with him or her to come up with a more amicable outcome and then say, "Good job!" But please, don't declare your kid to be *special!* Consider the words in the Constitution; everyone is equal in the eyes of the law, but at the same time we are not noted as being *special*. We all can use a bit of restraint.

The Gap: And another thing: let's talk about the generation gap. In the past, the association between people of every other generation, such as between a grandparent and grandchild, proved to be more balanced than the association between those of successive generations, such as a parent and child. This human behavior has been around since way back when. Unfortunately, the gap now includes the grandparents. Part of the problem started with telling children they are special. During their growing-up years, these special kids demonstrate superiority over adults, other kids, and even the house pet. After all, the adults are *not* special; therefore, the special kid doesn't have to listen to them. Another element is dancing around the idea of compromise. This alone is tearing families apart, causing them to become increasingly out of balance. That's because special people don't have to compromise. We all live on this planet, so let's get along together, build friendly relations, and forget this *special* label. Okay, I'll get off my soapbox, for now.

Goal Five: Principles, refinement, sophistication: these skills are achievable with *time* and effort!

It is thrilling when adults and children alike try new things as they attempt to comprehend their ethical and indisputable potentials. The lifelong thrill of tapping into my own potential and amassing countless skills and wisdom for refinement has no equal, and seventy-eight years later I'm still discovering new things. Oh, bother.

Callous people reveal the inevitable; the willingness to trample on the toes of others creating a race of people who are less than healthy and caring right here at home and abroad. Like everything under the sun, this one has a most menacing dark side. The devastating consequence is out-and-out war, which is never the answer. In a more socially conscious society, the disruption of people's lives by those who have devious and cavalier attitudes is continually monitored by the law and those who enforce it.

Physical as well as mental suffering affect people way beyond the intended target. This is un–American!

Disturbing aftereffects, caused by the perpetrators, produce brazen negativity in people and have a far-reaching impact on the rest of society. Since refinement is a learned skill, children have not yet had the time to understand how their words and actions affect others in harmful ways. But then, on the flip side, we need to know when to let those words and actions roll off our backs. This way, we can control threats aimed directly or indirectly at us. The potential for abusive attitudes will continue off into the future. A case in point is the television show in which children are in competition with other children as sophisticated chefs. I see this as exploitation of our youth. Please remember that sophistication is a learned skill and takes time to develop. As time progresses, our kids will get there through exposure to a myriad of positive and healthy activities within the family and the community. American families provide their children with precious time to *develop* into responsible thinkers and doers. However, placing your kid in the limelight (the *special* category) at such an early age will only foster conceit, uncaring, and bully-mindedness. As parents, we need to nurture our children in various ways:

- Give kids ample breathing space so they can find their voices at home.
- Teach children to recognize bad behavior, remember, your family council is a democracy.
- Allow them to develop and maintain their socially conscious personalities.
- Avoid burdening children with a narrow look on life.

And we must quit overtly pushing our youth! I think the evil groups causing mayhem in the Middle East are a prime example of how youth turns out when they receive narrow stimuli while growing into adulthood, if they make it that far in life.

Adults can easily propagandize youth into living a *special* lifestyle, convincing the children to behave like they are above the rest of us. A negative drawback is that kids sometimes break the rules before they know what the rules are about. You could blame this on the inner child acting up because his or her *social skills* haven't developed yet. Keep in mind that our kids are constantly watching and learning from the adult's actions and words. This is a natural way of learning. However, after growing up believing they are special, young adults hold a sense of entitlement to verbally abuse other adults. And the cycle continues. This is not good.

Regarding another arena needing guidance, the parents, as children's first teachers, should invest time in discussing the negative messages being sent over the airwaves. I know it seems to be an impossible task while raising children. Nobody said it would be easy! There's no bed of roses for us to lay our weary heads. So put on your thinking cap early, start when your child is one day old, and come up with ways to guide him or her away from unacceptable behaviors throughout your kid's development into adulthood. Remember the phone call I got from my pretend grandson? This is one example of objectionable behavior. Make *acceptable* conduct attractive because the opponents are doing their best to persuade kids to misbehave.

Here's another one of my pet peeves: when having fun, adults pepper their communication among themselves with insults. This confuses children and at the same time glorifies fun with insults. It's not nice to confuse kids; they will probably grow up never trusting anyone. Curtail insults when children are present, and do it in the spirit of democracy. Transparency comes to mind, so figure out other ways to have fun when children are present. Or just don't be in the same vicinity with children. It's your choice.

Whatever adults do and say, children will imitate. With that said, it saddens me when adults cannot see what comes of their off-putting actions and words. Here's an old phrase you might adopt as your mantra: "Look before you leap!" Bear in mind that youngsters have not lived long enough to understand the troubles they are about to inflict on themselves as well as many others as they mimic misbehaving adults. Maybe one solution would be to slow down just a bit! This can afford you time to *think*. It is not necessary to go at the speed of light.

Living a life in harmony is possible not only inside the family home but within the neighborhood, the city government, the state government, and eventually the national government. Did you notice I did not include the world? At present, we need to inspire the family to be active and informed voting citizens here at home. Keep your thoughts for world peace for another day. Before we get to that elevated level, ask yourself what you can do to steer your child away from destructive behaviors at home and school.

**Rule Eleven:** During council, never interrupt the person who is speaking. On the other hand, talking loudly, stuttering, or taking a whole lot of time saying nothing isn't any better.

Goal Six: Electronic etiquette: maintain an address. How can I attend your party if you don't have a "brick and mortar" address?

- The electronic world is turning American people away from maintaining a home address. That's not a good thing.
- Cell phones are aiding and abetting the practice of multitasking. "What's wrong with texting and driving?" you might ask. Or if your attention is averted on the subway or bus, you might miss the suggestive stare coming from a stranger directed toward your child. That sends shivers up my spine.
- Cell phones are connecting people all day long, all night long, all week long. When do we get a break to rest our thumbs and our eyes?
- Human contact is missing due to the single-mindedness of the *e-* this and *i-* that. This isn't such a good idea.
- All your eggs (phone, TV, camera, calendar, etc.) are going into one basket, so to speak. This could cause concern when there is no signal or, even worse, if the cell towers fall prey to terrorists.
- Cell towers are sitting ducks, like the off-season amusement park. That's scary.
- Dispatchers at 9-1-1 call centers can't locate you when you use a cell phone; a landline is grounded, but a cell phone is transient. Whether this is bad or good is debatable.
- We are growing into a generation of handicapped people using the texting mode of communication. What's pathetic is that nearly all the messages sent through texting have the potential to be misleading, as they very often are. Now, I'm not advocating that we return to carving our impactful messages in stone. That requires too much precious time and skill, and the modern person's tolerance for that is nonexistent.
- Two things differentiate humans from animals: we have a verbal and written language, and we have functioning thumbs. Ideas and dreams are created by humans. This is good.
- Texting is robbing us of a significant communication skill, language, and at the same time rendering useless our valuable thumbs. That's a double whammy! Giving so much attention to our cell phones isn't such a good idea.
- What I want to know is how men with large hands can punch the tiny keys correctly.

Goal Seven: Demonstrate the honesty, respect, and willingness to walk in the other guy's shoes and then maybe take a time-out.

You already have ownership of a safe forum during council, your home, where the family citizens can bring forth budding problems. Giving the benefit of the doubt and respecting other people *are* honest endeavors. If a council derails, take a good look at the other guy's point of view before tempers mushroom out of control. And *no* finger pointing, please!

Goal Eight: Set aside one council where citizens can participate in a debate on the meaning of power.

We are continually faced with a double-sided problem: big government is in bed with mega corporations and their bankers. The voting citizens, within your Family Political Council must be resolute and ready to build a strong and dignified presence not just for your children to adopt but for all council citizens. Power must not be coerced. Military personnel, business middle managers, college professors, airline pilots, union workers, tailors, firefighters, and even cowboys rounding up the herd all possess political powers. (You should try spending a day in the cowboys' boots as they lasso steers—builds character.) Offer gladly whatever capacity, skills, and the time you have and then work things toward an agreeable conclusion for all involved. I recommend adopting the following practices towards this aim: with a healthy posture, sit down; take several moments to lower your shoulders; release the tension in your jaw; and open your hands, placing them palms-up on your thighs. We owe it to ourselves to at least undertake this activity daily. That's power!

Use your guaranteed powers to get back your quality of life! Each American family citizen has the duty to observe the federal, state, and city governing bodies and local school boards in action. One night, I was privileged to sit in the audience to hear a question-and-answer session with the candidates of my local school board and city council. One candidate whom I thought was not worthy of holding a position on the board turned out to be exactly what the board needed. Politics—you've got to love it! It's important to identify both sides of an issue. Do this for every election. Develop your own Family Political Council so you can enter the voting booth confidently and know you have been heard. This is called flexing your political muscle. Families across America who participate in the governing of our country can expect the utmost pleasure in being Americans. "But money controls everything," you say. Maybe, but votes *can* eclipse money! Be proud of the red, white, and blue!

*American citizens* own the government and all its powers. *American citizens* merely loan the power to the legislators.

Goal Nine: Set-up workshops in your Family Political Council

Ask senior citizens in your neighborhood or coworkers you trust who have experienced government issues to speak at one of your Family Political Councils. By now, I'm assuming your council is established. This can be a fruitful experience. To avoid a potential gripe session, take the following steps:

1. Qualify your potential speaker's topic. Unless you are prepared for a fight, try to avoid topics that are too hot to handle. Example: escalating the defense budget.
2. Suggest that the speaker write a ten-minute speech about the matter he or she experienced, such as a city council meeting, a visit to the state capital, or an issue dealing with an overzealous city employee.
3. Encourage your guest speaker to be specific. Alert the speaker that your council citizens will be asking pertinent questions.

The possibilities abound! Tread lightly on this one; you want to emphasize the facts. Remember Joe Friday's statement: "Just the facts, ma'am!"

Goal Ten: Empower future voting citizens with honor and humility

Children supported by their families through regularly scheduled councils have the potential to grow up and be empowered, honest voting citizens with high standards and a good work ethic. With the help of the adults, extended family members come in handy here. Children benefit greatly by facing their personal issues within the family. However, should the children's zeal prompt adults to snicker at what they determine is silly and not worth listening to, remember that making fun of your kids' missteps is on the order of bullying and will serve to keep them at odds with the adults.

Lately, dysfunctional families appear to be the norm. Talk about a bland life with no growth! However, as you talk with one another, your council citizens can improve their chances of avoiding the dreaded and all-too-common family separation mishaps. I get goose bumps just thinking about the uplifting possibilities waiting for positive discoveries within the family. Please hold the thought that your humor can turn on a dime in so many negative ways when casually directed at children.

Another incentive I had for writing *Keep Voting, America* was mainly to help people become politically savvy in the following areas:

- The blatant disregard that past politicians demonstrated toward the citizens and our Constitution was prevalent in the twentieth century. In the wee, small hours of the twenty-first century, ruthless indifference toward the voting citizen is being flaunted in our faces by too many people in power *at every level.*
- Public office holders have no right to pass illegal laws and amendments to our Constitution that set the stage to weaken the voters' input. We must stop this tendency.
- Past and current presidents as well as Congress have slipped IOUs into the Social Security treasure chest. I say *treasure chest* because I, among millions of other retirees, treasure the forward thinking of President Franklin D. Roosevelt and his merry men for setting up the Social Security payment system we know as FICA. Just because we retired citizens are old doesn't mean we are no longer capable. Heck, no—we draw from the experiences of our lives as we keep an eagle eye on the governing of this great country we love. Hallelujah! People can't do this if they have one foot hovering over a grave and the other on a banana peel, now can they?
- Parents in past generations prepared their children for a smooth transition into adulthood. Not so much today.
- American citizens need to question where the money trail leads after the elections. This is where transparency is lacking!
- Let's include in this list the news reporters. Too many don't know how to ask pertinent questions. They dwell on the fluff or sensational questions. Yuck!

Goal Eleven: Follow the money!

Could it be that the lawmakers are writing legislation only for the citizens with big bucks, leaving all the rest of the voters out of the equation? Legislation is written for whom? *Follow the money!*

Goal Twelve: Serve up a plate of politics.

This is a lot to serve your family after dinner. But don't go overboard in the beginning! Avoid arranging more than one meeting a week; otherwise, it will get stale very quickly. Instead, set up citizens' committees. Take each element and work through the details toward an equitable conclusion. And be forthcoming when you need help. Ask, and the worst thing you will get is a no. Work on one element at a time and present the conclusions to the entire council in understandable English, a vital component for refining your Family Political Council.

I'll offer another suggestion for your consideration. I'm bringing this to the table because literacy is near and dear to me. I am a former volunteer English reading tutor at my local public library. The libraries could use your help, so volunteer to be a tutor. On the other hand, it is very likely that you know a family member or friend that is unable to read. Call your local library and ask how learning to read will have a positive impact on your friend's life. Many libraries have a one-on-one program for adults as well as children in or out of school. Going through the program is a positive, life-changing process. And it is free! Remember, above all else, there is to be *no finger pointing* should any member of your council be illiterate—*period!* And, forcing this program on anyone is out of the question.

Goal Thirteen: Manage your time.

The number 13 gets a bad rap. You might adopt positive actions and thoughts toward this number and turn those dreaded events, which might not happen, into an uplifting affair.

I realize that in today's economy, parents are stretched to the breaking point. Maintaining loyalty to both job and family is a fine line to traverse. This leaves little if any time for teaching children to be civic minded. The family breadwinner, working as an employee or operating a business, needs every ounce of energy and attention just to pull together a sensible living. (When I say sensible living, look around your house and assess how much stuff you own. And be honest—you may be living beyond a *sensible living* standard.) There are citizens who elect to work long hours or hold two or three jobs so they can stay ahead of the bill collector while continuing to buy stuff. Unfortunately, their family quality time suffers because there just isn't any more time for family. Stuff! Family quality time! Which one will you choose? One complaint that family breadwinners might express, "Relearn the Constitution? Absolutely no way do we have time for such frolicking!"

Here's a sad note: some job hunters have given up on ever finding decent-paying employment. As they drop out of the job market, the unemployment figures are dropping as well. Now we have a huge number of citizens with too much time on their hands. The result is that people are hopelessly lost. Time has become their enemy. But time can be your ally when *managed well*. And because you have *Keep Voting, America* in hand, ready to hoist your sails and get to the business of holding the politicians and yourself accountable, your days will be filled with uplifting books to read, letters to write, good fights to fight, and precious liberties to fetch back. Yeah, team! Push 'em back, push 'em back, waaay back!

About ten minutes before you turn out the lights tonight, check in with each family member to make sure they are okay, in person or, if you are away from home, on your smartphone or computer. Be prepared to hold it to just ten minutes; otherwise, it might turn into an all-nighter! It could be fun, but let's be responsible, especially if tomorrow is a school day.

Are we so absent minded that we are repeating the sixteenth and seventeenth centuries when the despots were in power in Europe? Have the tyrants changed their clothes? Has taxation without representation re-appeared in the twenty-first century? The one sizable difference today is that we don't have a huge body of water between the citizens and the oppressors. The terrorists are here walking, working, even planning our demise right here on the streets where we live. I don't say this to get you paranoid, on the contrary, I encourage all US citizens to be aware of your surroundings.

Goal Fourteen: Be aware of how language changes as you read historical letters.

For example, what is up with the phrase "all *men* are"? Does this include the fat guy, the Asian woman, and the high school drop-outs? *US citizens* includes everyone, but too often folks are left out of all sorts of social and professional arenas in America. And another question, why do some otherwise contemporary people still think that women and people of color are incapable of doing things? I can name a few examples.

- running the government
- fighting for freedom and our country
- leading the church
- learning the game of chess
- controlling the family purse strings
- becoming mathematicians and scientists
- operating a business

This is especially prevalent in the military, where, in many cases, the white male GIs get promoted but not the "other" GIs. Women and other minorities are forced to accept total disrespect. *Criminal!*

We all need to make life in America better by supporting an *equal rights amendment*. Do you understand what *equal rights* means? Be honest! Now that you have started your Family Political Council, accepting other people's offerings can become the norm.

Each family citizen possesses unique skills, such as the awareness of how things work and don't work, a willingness to ask pertinent questions, and an eagerness to suggest helpful solutions. I hope you are beginning to see the value of participating in government. And while you're at it, spruce up your language, it's getting raunchy. I think I forgot what port of entry I was headed for! Oh, well, the view of my American flag waving atop of the flag pole is nice.

Goal Fifteen: Be truly free to function democratically in your own home!

As you form your council, the gathering together may be an arduous undertaking. Fortunately for the living today, we have a blue-print for setting up a government. Families and neighbors can be suspicious of one another, just like the citizens who formed the United States of America in the eighteenth century. By following the guidelines in this book, each member of your political family will have the power to make and prolong their promise to do good things morally as well as socially. It must be the goal of all core citizens, the American family, to be truly free to function well in their daily lives, not to be a ward of the state and not to be dominated by an autocratic or military head of household. Working together to do the right things within the family and then the greater society of America is a worthwhile goal. How wonderful it will be to advance all the citizenry above the welfare state!

Speaking of welfare, many people "on welfare" seem to have an abundance of time on their hands. Establishing a Family Political Council might promote, at the least, good time management like serving a nutritious dinner at the table each night at the same time. Now you have time to read the constitutional amendments and become trustworthy stewards. How about that? You have set an attainable goal. I dare you to fight the good fight for liberty. Remember, this is a free society, and all citizens need to be responsible for their actions and words. Thus, you are free to do the following:

- speak without reprisal in the spirit of goodwill, as in "I dare you ..."
- worship privately or in established religions, as you wish
- follow your dreams, as long as they don't rain on my parade
- keep government domination away
- move about freely in this vast country of ours
- seek out other citizens who are like minded about liberty

A hypothetical dialogue among neighbors about the above topics in the family council could go like this:

Citizen A: "Speaking without reprisal? This concept is tough to navigate."

Citizen B: "What about peer pressure coming at us from all angles?"

Citizen A: "That's enough to strike anyone deaf, dumb, or dead."

Citizen C: "The risk of being on the receiving end of a fist or gun is not a risk taken but a way of life."

Citizen B: "Moving away may alleviate the problem for a while if you have the money to do it."

Citizen A: "Even if you did get away, where human nature is concerned we tend to take attitudes like fear or aggression right along with us. Let's think of this as not an option. We want to eliminate as many fears and aggressive attitudes as possible."

Citizen C: "So what else can people do?"

Citizen B: "Some people act crazy."

Citizen A: "This might help keep the baddies away, but it's not an option, either."

Citizen C: "How about developing the attitude of forgiveness and becoming responsible for the words we speak and the actions we take?"

Citizen A: "Now you are using your head. Can you pull this off?"

Citizen B: "There's always the tack of suggesting to help offenders with their English or maybe inviting them to supper."

Citizen A: "Supper? The nasty people can look at this in a couple of ways: (1) you are weak and could be taken down in a flash; or (2) maybe the nasty person will take the high road and be grateful someone respects and trusts them in their home."

Citizen B: "Without a doubt, *we must not promise anything* we cannot deliver."

Citizen A: "Be sure to think carefully and weigh the options before attempting to show how caring people can be."

Citizen B looks at Citizen C: "What say we give this 'go unplugged once a week council' thing a try?"

Reason, compromise, new information and hope for a better day all work together.

Goal Sixteen: Validate your dialogue.

I'm offering four valuable books to help individual family citizens further their mental and social fitness at council.

*Book One: Robert's Rules of Order.* Refer to this book often. Interrupting others while they are talking is troublesome in any conversation. The person speaking may lose their train of thought, rendering their input to the conversation null and void. This has happened to me on many occasions. I've often wondered if the person interrupting me is aware of it, and if so, whether he or she cares, or maybe he is filling the shoes of a bully! Everybody wants to be heard, but it is the other person's turn. Everyone wants to talk about how much they know, but did you ever think that your opinions may be unfavorable or unwanted? I'm involved in a robust book club, and a story we read was about oppression. Our group leader asked each one of us to describe what the word *oppression* meant to us. One woman, who was foreign born, spoke up loudly about the horrendous things people do to one another, belaboring gory details. I stopped her by saying louder, "Enough!" She glared at me but yielded the floor. Later, a couple of us spoke to her on why she was hushed keeping her from deliberating further. Unfortunately, she did not get it. Her response was that she intended to defend her First Amendment right to the death, if necessary, and she never apologized to the group. Today, freedom of speech is not in imminent danger. If coming forth with abundant details brings distress to people, then drop the details. They are unwanted. In my defense for using the phrase "robust book club," funny and spirited debate is most desirable. Gore is not.

Another area of concern to me is the television programming on which political advisors, newspaper columnists, and talk-show participants speak loudly enough to drown out the other contributors. Subsequently, their messages get jumbled up. All too often, the studio audience members come to blows. It becomes a free-for-all and only paves the way for a breakdown in communication. We, the TV viewers, have the last laugh, so to speak. If we are watching a program on TV and the message becomes obscured, we can easily pick up the remote and change the channel. In council, don't go overboard when it is your time to talk. Nobody likes to be completely left out of the gossip, heart to heart, dialogue, banter, chin-wagging, discussion, tête-à-tête, chat, gab, conversation, utterance, debate, yak, chitchat, exchange, negotiation, confession, or natter. (Words are so much fun when used appropriately.)

- *Books 2 and 3: Dictionary and thesaurus.* Keeping in mind your mental fitness, another couple of excellent books to own and refer to would be the dictionary and thesaurus. Zeroing in on the appropriate word to convey your exact message is paramount in completing your dialogue. I have fun using the thesaurus when choosing juicy words that aptly convey my message. Develop your determination and perseverance, and play word games such as Scrabble. Using these two books stimulates the players toward a thrilling and spirited competition. An added benefit, your vocabulary will increase handsomely and you will become a better speller. Your English teacher will applaud your efforts!

- *Book 4: Etiquette books.* Now for a social fitness exercise: refer to a book on etiquette. It sounds lame, but you might keep an open mind while exploring *Keep Voting, America.* You will be surprised how relevant etiquette teachings are in politics, local through national and even worldwide. Also, being mindful of the rules of etiquette can possibly get you out of some sticky and potentially harmful situations. Caution: some people will charm the pants off you with their civil manners. Don't be fooled by their shameless message. Following are several synonyms for *etiquette: protocol, custom, propriety, decorum, politeness, good manners.* Gosh, so many fabulous words to work with! There's no need to shove the English language aside to use four-letter words.

Remember the phrase "Do no harm." One application of this phrase is using language unsuitably around children—well, anybody for that matter. If four-letter words are uttered, the potential for creating a *dual log* (instead of a dialogue) that will send the conversation out of control and into a shouting match that can lead to physical harm is real, all because you chose to use less-than-appropriate language. Besides, I would much rather be completely understood than run the risk of getting a black eye. If you do get a black eye, don't count on having legal grounds for a battery charge. Foul language is vented too liberally in the twenty-first century, not to mention that annoying *beep* repeated often on TV and movies, almost every other word. One might argue, "Let's drop the *beep* and unmask the four-letter words as we talk *at* one another. Or we could use appropriate language and have clarity whenever we talk *with* one another." Now we don't need the beep. My choice is to clean up our conversational language. What say you? These pathetically overused, empty words that people toss out like dirty water can affect the very young, tarnishing their minds and reinforcing negative behavior as they grow up. Catch a very few moments of *reality* television and you will see what I am talking about. But, on occasion, a well-planned four-letter word, like *damn,* can convey your discontent and make it perfectly clear that you do not approve of bad behavior. (Please note I said *discontent* and not *anger.* There is too much anger expressed; in its place, we can demonstrate discontent, a much more malleable emotion to express.) *Please use caution!*

Because children are eager to copy adults, they will pick up whatever words you say, and how you say them, as well as the actions you take. If we express four-letter words as appropriate, we turn our backs on the ideal of doing no harm. Raising our voices and abruptly ending the conversation could set the stage for the discussion to end in violence. Wisely chosen words can keep feathers from flying and making a mess all over the place. "I'm not cleaning them up!"

Let me set the record straight: I am *not* a Goody Two–shoes. Moreover, I'm not above carrying on a spirited and meaningful conversation. Keep in mind that kids will imitate adults. Imitation is the greatest form of flattery, whether it's in a positive way or not. That said, adults need to take the time to think before putting their foot in their mouth! At all times, it is imperative to honor other citizens comments. Throughout your Family Political Council, this rule will enhance everything your council endeavors to accomplish. You really don't want to reveal your ignorance, do you? But still, it's your choice.

Take a gander at Ben Franklin's "Rules for Making Oneself a Disagreeable Companion". You might get a chuckle out of it, as well as a better understanding of how people look when dominating a conversation. Check it out on the internet under: B. Franklin's four rules for Disagreeable people.

> **Rule twelve:** Before you voice a complaint, think
> of at least 2 or 3 possible solutions to the
> problem. This will elevate your statue,
> making you part of the answer,
> not part of the problem!

Goal Seventeen: Discuss term limits for all offices

Establishing the Family Political Council can be productive while solidifying your steadfast efforts for maintaining your constitutional liberties, but only if you work at it. Starting with your second month's council, the mayor will spearhead the proceedings for the future—that is, until he or she is voted out of office. Discuss term limits for all offices. When continuing your council past the exploratory period, be aware that any elected position such as mayor is to be offered to *all* citizens over the age of eighteen. If you accept people other than family, encourage them to run for an office as well. There will be no career mayors in this family council, thank you very much! In the future, you might set a minimum age for certain offices such as congressional page, a position that can be held by kids at least five years old, depending on their level of social interaction. In the beginning of their term of office, an adult may perhaps accompany the child when delivering messages. Gosh, another teaching opportunity. As you progress with your council, write legislation regarding how long a citizen is to serve in any one office—say, six months. The rest is up to you. And please remember that this is a democracy.

To improve your time management, allow yourself a few minutes a day to read US history. Time yourself for about fifteen to twenty minutes and select a quiet environment where you can concentrate on what you are reading. Weather permitting, the backyard would be nice, or sip a cup of coffee at a sidewalk café. Do this several times each week. Avoid any bedtime reading, as it might keep you up for hours. Try this for a couple of weeks, and if it's working for you, continue for a couple more weeks. A habit is forming. Good habits can save you tons of time reinforcing you to get tons of things done. Besides, fifteen minutes is such a short amount of time—just 0.010416666 percent of your day. Rather minuscule, don't you think? My figures may be a bit off, but don't fire me, please!

Goal Eighteen: Go the extra mile when you can.
The following items are optional but could be beneficial:

- Use a lectern or music stand for ease when offering speeches. It could do double duty as the voting booth.
- For your future council's clarification, a camcorder could come in handy. Remember, our objective is to carry on a professional council where real work gets done in a no-nonsense fashion. The camcorder can someday reveal painful and embarrassing words or actions that can bite you in the—well, you know what! Please don't use your cell phone for this purpose.

Goal nineteen: Set a few standards and then hold yourself to higher ones.
Take everything into consideration: dress code, punctuality, polite behavior, appropriate language, using healthy posture while sitting in council, and even asking for help when you get stuck. All these activities will further your efforts as you take care of those annoying problems you experience every day, all while learning our political past. We are all in this boat together. When the "weather" gets rough, some hands can paddle and some hands can bail. Sounds like positive reciprocity to me! What say you?

Notes and dates recorded:

# CHAPTER 17

## Pay forward social skills from one generation to the next

Treasured family teachings can be antisocial messages or honest, law-abiding lessons. Let's contrast what comes from these opposing principles. Consider moralistic, thoughtful, and joyful ideals compared to hatred, distrust, greed, lies, and public sex acts.

What do we get if we follow one or the other? Which category will lead to the ruination of our country? Which one will advance the United States? Will American citizens be kept in limbo, resulting in little if any progress or hope for the future?

Go ahead and break down each word in the two examples. After all, if we don't understand the individual words, then how can we expect to glean the concept of the full messages? Study and talk with one another in council about what words mean. Don't get into the habit of glazing over words and ideas just because the subjects are not familiar or are *uncomfortable.*

Everyone in council doesn't necessarily have to go along with what is conveyed. Instead, learn to agree to disagree; this keeps the conversation lively and not detrimental to your life and limb. Here's a trick question: Is the gathering together of two or more people while talking about opposing concepts considered politics? Can you follow this concept? It's within your ability. But leave emotions outside the door and down the block; we have no time for flare-ups during council. Just in case, be sure you have the no-finger-pointing sign handy.

## A rational mind instead of the loony farm

There was a time when courtesy and moral convictions were passed down through each American family: rich or poor, young or old, religious or not, single race or a mix of races, and the many unique cultures around the world. Years ago, the passing of both the moral and courtesy batons secured the vital connection from generation to generation. Unfortunately, for many present-day families, this fundamental link is missing. Maybe the children feel their parents' versions of courtesy and moral behaviors are too mundane. In the latter part of the twentieth and the beginning of the twenty-first centuries, many children had no clue that precious treasured family lessons ever existed.

Could it be that the drug companies, entertainment and advertising industries, and the government, supported by the uncaring, powerful money people, have taken up the slack by inundating everyone with constant anti-American family messages depicting over-the-top greed; the ruination of the American language, *English;* public sex acts; and excessive alcohol, drugs, foul language, and tobacco ads aimed directly at all generations? Even documentaries have power over the general population. I have watched many documentaries and afterward felt I had wasted my time. They seem to get the doomsday message right, but they do not offer any alternative to, say, fix the sinkholes appearing with frequency. The sinkhole swallowed up the house! Gasp!

And then there is the hatred toward anyone and distrust toward everyone. These elements in some form or another have been around for centuries. Be that as it may, we don't need *excessive* greed or *public* sex acts. (I'm not talking nudity. Come on, nudity is a form of freedom. What we don't need are sex acts flaunted in the public eye while participants are partially or completely nude. This is for consenting adults in private, and *never* for children.) We do not need hatred or distrust tearing relationships apart, nor do we need the communications tools that are constantly in our faces. I guess that, for some, all the above antisocial behaviors, when acted out, could be misconstrued as an adrenaline rush, but at what expense to human decency and trust? Picture an image of two little figures, one each sitting on your left and right shoulders, respectfully. Think of them as the middlemen or prime movers. One character drags you into the sex dens and dark, dank allies where the drug dealers operate, but the other character picks you up and carries you past all that inhumane sorrow. No body needs a village to perform a sex act!

What I am about to say causes me much discomfort, but I'm duty-bound to continue. Falling down drunk while embracing all you are hoarding at the same time, flaunting sex acts as you tear down the English language, and exhibiting distrust and hatred towards all authority—is this the new American way of life? Instead, let's talk politics!

No society is perfect. However, our Constitution encourages the US citizens to "strive for a more perfect union." For us, the *journey* is much more satisfying than reaching perfection. Why bother? What is left after perfection? Nothing!

So many different races and ethnic groups are screaming to be heard, corrupt money people are wanting more, and don't forget the female and male disputes. It's enough to send anyone to the loony farm.

- First, think acceptance.
- Second, allow others to dream and follow their dreams.
- Third, give your hard-earned money until it hurts.
- Fourth, be aware of how your choices affect other people.
- Fifth, live and let live.

A rational mind realizes there are problems with these five points.

First, acceptance is a good start, but how much acceptance is necessary before a person loses his or her identity? Acceptance starts as soon as we do something simple like relaxing enough to calm our breathing. This will give us time to look at the other guy's viewpoint.

Second, what about the person who is determined to own us by taking away our dreams? Confront this person with firmness, but don't go overboard by giving into anger or you might lose it all.

Third, why do we have to give our hard-earned money until it hurts? Try volunteering or donating some of that stuff you are hoarding. (Please do me a favor: be honest about your dollar worth and the number of shoes you have in your four-hundred-square-foot closet.) Check out charitable organizations. Do this with your children, but choose wisely so that you don't put your kids at risk. Acceptable examples are a church soup kitchen and the reading program in your public library. I prefer to work with organizations where I get to offer the help directly rather than send money. If you choose to get involved with a fund-raising event, make sure it is valid and legal.

Fourth, if you are involved with group A and it is hell-bent on destroying group B so it can get all the things that group B has, that's scary for group B, having targets painted on their backs. Again, confront the aggressors firmly and stand your ground. On second thought, ease into the activity of standing your ground.

Fifth, there was a time when people were overly concerned about others, and their continual worry created health hazards like stomach ulcers. My dad always said he didn't have ulcers; he gave them. But seriously ...

Greed rules people and leads them to abuse these five ideals. Heck, kids in the neighborhood clash with kids down the street. Married couples have their moments;

hundreds of job hunters dishonestly compete for one job. That's enough to get anyone's fists up. "Le-me-a-um!"

I recently felt like this, but the exercise of taking steady breaths cleared my mind and allowed me that vital moment to come up with an amicable solution.

Anxiety reigns supreme variety of woes. Heads of multiple gods are added which god is trustworthy? There's no easy answer, we Americans want to life, we need each family together once a week, Keep the sign with the handy in case the citizens

among US citizens from a states have failed. Even the to this mixed bag. But I don't know the answer. but I know one thing: if hold on to our quality of to go unplugged, gather and *talk with one another.* blaming finger crossed out cause a raucous. The

sign's message will be worth hundreds of times its weight in goodwill.

I hope I have kindled your sense of wonderment to continue your council meetings once a week and talk politics with one another.

## Treasured family teachings at home

Picture a kindergarten child with a runny nose wiping his nose with his hand and then immediately running to the teacher and reaching for her h—*stop!* To get that image out of your head, let's enter the family home, where the parents have offered just one of the millions of treasured family lessons to their children. The above situation could have been avoided if the parent of the sniffling child had taken the time in a most pleasant way and in their *home* to teach the child to use a tissue and then toss said tissue into the trash. Let's keep basic cleanliness learning in the home.

Notes and dates recorded:

## Other ethnic family teachings

In America, vast numbers of people of different ethnicities follow their own traditions and teachings. After all is said and done, this is what constitutes America in all its glory. Throughout history as well as today, thousands and thousands of immigrants have matriculated into our society. Elements of their traditions will fade away, and some will be embraced by the general population. Because we are a great big melting pot, Americans need to appreciate the value of each ethnic group rounding out our society. On one hand, we continually follow traditions. On the other, we have become a world leader through innovation and responsibility. Harmony, innovation, and responsibility go together extremely well when citizens work at it. But how can we trust people when we don't understand their traditions? Does your tradition fly in the face of my tradition? Which traditions are worth following? Do you want to harm me? American citizens' central concern is *peace*. Tradition and change have every right to coexist in the name of friendship. We have it in us to make it so. Do you agree?

Many of the world citizens have fled their homelands because of the warmongers taking over their lands, their homes, and their very lives. The United States, along with many other countries, has implemented trade agreements and is now taking in refugees. Because of the trade agreements in the ravaged countries, the United States and its allies have a vested interest in the welfare of the afflicted citizens.

Getting to know other traditions through education must continue for all Americans. If you do not want to go through the process of learning other cultures for whatever reason, then before you speak out against a culture, ask yourself if what you are going to say shows insincerity towards other peoples beliefs. Then try to refrain from voicing negative opinions. This is where many conflicts fester and later become problematic for all concerned. And for what? Agreeing to disagree will give you time to maybe learn about the other guy's treasured cultural teachings. If you do this, everyone will have a better chance of accepting your side of the story. Believe it or not, acceptance is paramount.

Here at home (in the United States), we try to exercise compassion toward the endless marches of refugees around the globe. I don't know what else we as Americans can do, but I sure don't want opposing traditions erasing my well-being.


## What tears us apart?

In my growing-up years, I lived in three states: Oklahoma, Arizona, and California. With the help of my parents, through a tried-and-true moral value system and twelve years in the Girl Scouts, I learned to use several elements to solve problems. When it was my turn to raise a family, I possessed the wherewithal to inspire a life of ethical values. Honesty and principled lifestyles are rapidly giving way to out-of-control anger and something much more ruthless: immediate satisfaction. Living way beyond our means and paranoid that someone will take all that stuff away from us are elements of an out-of-control lifestyle. What a slippery slope.

But I feel that the major element tearing families apart emerges in the form of the mass media, which is driven by technology and money people, of course. The relentless growth of the entertainment and news reporting industries is taking the personal teachings away from the children's parents. With the media's impersonal message breaking down the family values at an alarming rate, our children develop resentful attitudes toward all authority. One tragic state of affair is when young people are cut down before they have a chance to find out who they are. Another image comes to mind in the form of crowded courtrooms and prisons. Could the messages aimed at our American youth be compared to one self-appointed German chancellor in his quest for power as he crafted his inhumane Hitler Youth? At least he was upfront with his intentions. But then, regrettably, too many people turned a deaf ear to what became a horrifying tragedy of human dignity and ultimately death on a massive scale. As I write this book, a group of terrorists plotting the demise of the United States is gaining momentum.

*Why are they taking up space on this earth?*

I sincerely hope our president and Congress will come together and halt this intrusion. Heaven help us if they are unsuccessful.

Back to our children: kids under the voting age, which is eighteen, are misinterpreting what *liberty* means. Children claim that their knowledge is more up to date and complete compared to that of *older* folks living inside and outside their homes. Because of young people's superior attitude, expressing out-and-out resentment toward their parents and other adults is common. How many times have you heard, in a whiny voice, "That's not fair!" Ask your kids if they have heard of Stephen Hawking, the theoretical physicist living with amyotrophic lateral sclerosis, better known as ALS. Professor Hawking has no time for the "that's not fair" attitude. Instead, he is quoted as saying, "Life would be tragic if it weren't funny."

There is an almost impenetrable defiance reinforcing the breaking point in the parent–child relationship. When I was a teenager, I was convinced my parents were too old-fashioned and didn't know what a teenager's life was about. Silly me—they had been teenagers just a few years before me. Thank goodness, my family's ethical teachings were firmly wedged into my subconscious, cheering me on to grow into a responsible adult in spite of my youthful short-sightedness. American society will work better when children are not drenched in hatred toward their parents. The across-the-board decline of the American family, by and large, is liable for the huge decay of our liberties. The family's ship is listing dangerously out of balance with very little evidence of regaining composure, something akin to our senselessly top-heavy government. So what's your take on liberty?

Unless we begin demonstrating compassion with understanding and patience along with cheerfulness, the risk of sinking our ship in the treacherous storms can only increase. Both parent and child will get to their destination when all generations meet each other halfway, including, if you have them, aunts, uncles, grandparents, cousins, and so on. When we have a meeting of the minds, the escalating anger will be replaced with calm, allowing precious time to think of possible solutions to just about any trouble crossing our paths. Would you like to lose your ability to speak in public or associate freely with whom you wish? I talk about families, but there is a growing segment of society choosing to stay single; they have no plans for starting families. All too often, single people are left out of social gatherings. That's unfortunate because single people have dreams as well as problems to work out. I have been single for several decades and have found pleasure in volunteering as my community rep. Remember the referendum I mentioned earlier? I now have several friends with whom I can talk politics. Who knew I would be talking politics with so many people? Give the single citizen a chance to be heard.

If things get out of hand, you might consider these twelve elements:

1. Sit back in your chair and let your arms dangle at your side. Or,
2. Walk away temporarily.
3. Unplug your devices, leaving them behind just for a little while.
4. Breathe *rhythmically.*
5. Sit down and close your eyes (but eyes open while operating a vehicle, please).
6. Relax your shoulders.
7. Relax your hands.
8. Unlock your jaw.
9. Smile, sincerely, if you would be so kind.
10. Speak softly.

11. That doesn't mean to use your tiny inside voice; we want to hear what you have to say. Now everyone can begin to reduce the hostile environment.
12. We shouldn't have to build another twenty-foot-high wall!

About that wall, the president has expressed support for a transparent wall. I guess shatterproof glass is harder to scale than a chain-link fence.

Once more, I'm speaking out in protest of the lack of moralistic actions and deeds exhibited by individual citizens with and without suffrage. Folks in America have a couple of things in common: we are human beings with the potential to do the right thing, and we do it in the name of liberty. And then there are the turncoats who are unwilling to do anything without a monetary reward. Come on, guys and gal's—you can't allow money to dictate your every move. Remember the bad guys poised to take all your hard-earned money? That was a question!

Nevertheless, this book is addressed to American citizens, individuals as well as families. Here is a short list of citizens:

- federal, state, and city lawmakers
- the hardware store manager and his family
- vice presidents of corporations
- the counterperson at McDonalds and her daughter
- bank executives, their employees, and families
- the prisoners housed in the overcrowded jails and their estranged families
- everyday people instantly thrown into the limelight of fame
- welfare recipients
- babies born addicted to drugs
- Boy and Girl Scout leaders and their families
- American citizens, whether born or naturalized
- ranchers, farmers, their ranch hands, and yes, their families too
- veterinarians and their four-legged furry critters
- schoolteachers and their families
- American veterans

Forgive me if I didn't include you. An enlightened society is achievable now and in the future.

Think about truth versus fact. I want to engender a better understanding of these words. In my Thorndike-Barnhart Student Dictionary, copywrite © 1997, *truth* as a noun means "matter or circumstance as it really is; a fixed or established principle, law; proven doctrine; in a *general abstract sense* that which is real; nature of being true, exact, honest, sincere or loyal." The entry for the word *truthful* reads "agreeing with the facts."

From the same dictionary, *fact* is a noun from the Latin *factum* meaning "(thing) done; thing known to be true or to have really happened; *Many scientific facts are based on actual observations...*" The entry for *factual,* an adjective, says, "concerned with facts; actual; real."

Truth can be personal, meaning different things to different people. Remember the movie I mentioned earlier, *Vantage Point*? Facts, as they stand, can be proved. I would rather ask for facts than the truth when questioning eyewitnesses.

I find researching the meanings of words refreshing and enlightening when I suspect I have used them incorrectly. Try it—you might enjoy the process!

## Family values

Family values are not a pie-in-the-sky concept. When everyone exercises the moral duties of our country, we will thrive as a nation where the principles of liberty, truth, and justice are passed on to each succeeding generation. The children are a worthwhile endeavor, and so are their parents your extended family members and the immigrants living down the block. They can benefit from your family treasured teachings.

A sound approach for action comes in the form of investing in America's future through family values. One reliable way to invest in our socially conscious society is to restore parents and public-school teachers back into our children's educational equation.

## A quick word about government spending

Every day, another costly, monumental, historic event takes place, putting America even more firmly behind the economic eight ball. Early in 2015, hundreds of thousands of federally employed citizens received their pink slips because there wasn't enough money to run our government. For some, the layoff was temporary, about a half a day. But this was just enough to send many Americans into a state of distress. Could it be there are too many people working in government and too many public programs suffering from bad management? I'm tired of paying taxes for inferior workmanship and poor management, yet still they continue. Even worse, I'm tired of getting the runaround when I call for information about a public service. The response I commonly get is, "It's not my job, lady!" Boo!

## Another pathetic consequence

We must approach the moral side of our politicians. Perhaps we can carve a huge chunk off the country's debt by taking another look at the waste in government from the bottom up. Then maybe a greater majority of US citizens won't have to float a loan just to buy a week's worth of groceries. Rather pathetic, don't ya think? And this is America?

Plan well and do all three financial activities: invest, spend, and save!
Picture your wallet. Now see the kid's college fund flying out of it. Oh, dear!
Two agendas: one public, the other in the back room. Transparency, anyone?
Picture a see-saw with a house on one end and a pile of cash on the other.
Budget and expenses—where do I begin?

Notes and dates recorded:

# CHAPTER 18

Life, Liberty, and the Pursuit of a Happy and Industrious Life Isn't Going to Endure if We Continue Our Present Course of Action—or Inaction

## More family social education

In the past, people's values, including moral values, were successfully handed down through the family because the parents started their children's learning from the ripe ol' age of *one day*. Not on their first birthday or when they turn three years old, but before the newborn is welcomed into your home. A mother's voice is firmly implanted into the infant's brain, and hopefully the messages are kind and nurturing. There was a time when children, from birth to five or six years of age, were taught social skills in the home. As they matured, parents gradually widened the circle of social activities. Raising youngsters in America, parents or guardians are allowed the time to follow these traditional values.

Today, very young children are flooded with way too many externally generated inducements—for instance, resentment toward anyone who doesn't agree with them. They can't process these messages because young children haven't had the time to develop tolerance for overstimulation. Heck! Even adults struggle when subjugated to voluminous amounts of information. In the olden days, by the time children entered elementary school, they already possessed politeness and respect in their home and the immediate neighborhood. Next, this respect was passed on to their teachers, the school bus driver, the janitor, the cafeteria ladies, and the librarian. See how the circle of learning is gradually broadening? Regrettably, many children today lack these positive social qualities as they enter public school. Before exposing your kid to new avenues, so to speak, check it out to verify your choice is safe and uplifting.

## A second house of learning

The children's first established house of education wasn't built in the form of a battlefield. Classrooms are for learning important stuff like the English language, history, math, and maybe even wood shop. Tormenters in the form of bullies thrive in a school environment. I believe if we the parents, or grandparents, could 'roam the halls' of the schools and ferret out early on the bullies-- we could halt the continued torment inflicted on our children. But don't tell anyone this is your mission. We don't want the bullies to go underground. But then, we *must* use diplomacy during our witch hunt. Our aim is to *nurture* the bully while he grows up and encourage a path worthy of a *good citizen*. Can't do that if she goes underground. You might make an appointment with the principal and discuss a possible plan of action to reveal the problem children. Just a thought!

In your Family Political Council, talk about the uncomfortable results of being exposed to a bully. This will enable your kid to recognize a bully for what he or she is and encourage your child to seek help from adults in charge, such as a teacher or police officer. But please go easy on your actions and words to level the playing field; you don't want the superintendent to call you into the office. The story of *The Boy Who Cried Wolf* can provide an excellent lesson.

If our children are to grow into responsible voters, we, their parents or guardians, must demonstrate family values such as these:

- personal hygiene, all the way from shampooing your hair to clipping toenails
- social eating habits, such as using a knife and fork as intended and closing the mouth while chewing
- respect for authority, including parents, school principal, store clerks, police officers, and so on
- showing courtesy to everyone, even if you think you don't like them
- thinking before speaking

Can you think of more?

Remember the saying, "Imitation is the most sincere form of flattery." Your kid is copying your every move—good, bad, or indifferent. As adults, you must take part in an uplifting kind of lifestyle that is healthy, social, respectful, courteous, and wholesome. Articulate through proper English so that everyone involved can be on the same page. I would much rather live in a society where good behavior is the norm, setting aside the one person in ten thousand who *may* act out poorly. Let's right liberty's sails by changing our tack as we navigate the winds of moral values in our personal Family Political Council ship!

As a side note, when I was in the senior level of Girl Scouts, my troop chose to be mariners; hence my use of nautical terms in *Keep Voting, America*. Instead of using the term *troop* to define us, we were a ship. The ship's leader was our Skipper, the president was the OD (Officer of the Deck), the secretary was the yeoman, the assistant leader was the First Mate, and so on. I want to go on record about my twelve years in Girl Scouts to say that so much of what I learned through scouting is still with me today. (I was fortunate that both parents were active during my scouting experiences.) Quality of life was a big part of my upbringing. One of the most usable skills I gleaned through scouting was a keen sense of problem solving. Give scouting a try—both children and adults!

Notes and dates recorded:

# CHAPTER 19

## For the doubters

Maybe you feel there is no choice when it comes to the crooked politicians and the greedy corporate world, oh, but you do. Sail your council ship through the turbulent waters of government and seek the real reasons that we, as a nation, have lasted so long.

Consider the seventeenth- and eighteenth-century tyranny the colonists struggled with and the sacrifices they made for the sake of everlasting liberty. They did it for us, the current living citizens of the United States, and it is our turn to secure freedom for the future generations. Study government documents and the vast array of topics written by ordinary people published in books, magazines, newspapers, and a host of documentaries aired on television during the past two hundred and fifty years. Well, television came on board less than 75 years ago and the internet more recently: but you get my drift. That's a lot of research. Nevertheless, when all the citizens of your Family Political Council pitch in, the volumes of studying are within your means. Your voyage will continue to be a joyful crossing through life, where a boatload of wonderful discoveries will sustain you throughout your journey. It sounds rosy, but when one or two problems show up, your stamina will activate and demonstrate your resolve to carry on.

If you're a skeptic, hold off on your public denial and do some more reading. People are standing up for their rights by joining groups like Occupy Wall Street, which started on September 17, 2011, and lasted for a year. In 2017, groups like CREW demonstrated their unwillingness to "take it on the chin" from corporations, big banks, and congressional leaders who are out of touch with the people they are supposed to be representing.

Notes and dates recorded:

# CHAPTER 20

## The parental guardian

Parents take on the role as their children's first teachers. It is a daunting task because it is a lifelong commitment from the cradle through adulthood. In a perfect world, a solid education comes from truth, virtue, don't forget integrity, and then pause for a little humor.

These four elements encourage parents to pay forward basic respectful attitudes to their children. But do we mess up? Of course, we do! Frankly, time-tested values are being replaced with an ever-increasing tolerance for lies and distrust. And, yes, anger is keeping the family core citizens away from what has historically made Americans stand tall. Foolishly, the idea of being a stakeholder for liberty and justice for all has lost its luster. Think of two fellows beating the crap out of each other or two kids having fun while measuring ingredients to make their favorite cookies. Which one will you choose?

Families are shouting at each other, and no one is listening. I'm offering a couple of suggestions for a better quality of life: (1) Parents *must* set parameters so that children know what is expected of them and what they can expect from their parents. But here's a word of caution to parents: don't go overboard. Making too many rules too quickly can turn your kids against you. (2) When punishment is a necessity, make sure it fits the crime. Many years ago, while living in Hawaii, I fell under the spell of a con artist. The *Readers Digest* version is that he wrote a check to me on a closed account. It was the first time this ever happened to me—and the last time as well! The amount happened to be a little higher than my rent check amount. Unfortunately, *my* rent check was returned to me stamped "ISFs," indicating that I had insufficient funds in my account to cover the check. Regrettably, my son and I were evicted. Talk about a dark and gloomy night! However, being a responsible citizen, I tightened my belt, regained the money in a timely manner, and paid the delinquent rent. But (oh dear, there's that ever-prevalent *but*) no one was available to take my place at work; therefore, I had to rely on my ten-year-old child to take my twice-earned rent money, in cash, to the landlord. Being a kid, he stopped at the penny arcade and put all the money in the machines. *All the cash!* His punishment was to remain in his Skivvies, stay in the apartment, and drink only water and eat only bread for five days. Was this too severe? Well, he never did anything like that again.

I'm compelled to stop here for an additional word on learning to read. A formal education is great; however, education comes in many different forms. Learning through sight and hearing is one way of educating yourself, although it can be a bit slow and you must be in the right place at the right time. Then there's picking up a book and reading it. But it shouldn't be just any book. Leave the romance novels for another day. If an adult in your household can't read past the first-grade level, then do not pass "Go," do not collect two hundred dollars, head directly to your local public library, and *ask for an English reading tutor.* It's free! Now you have absolutely no excuse for not expanding your education through reading.

## Outside influence taking over the treasured family lessons

Unfortunately, ever since the 1950s, too many parents have allowed their children's education, social as well as academic, to come from the entertainment and advertising industries, over which the parents have utterly *no* control. In my teenage years, my family did not own a television, so I was exempt from this form of commercial education. I'm not talking about shows like *Sesame Street, Captain Kangaroo,* and *Mister Rogers' Neighborhood*—those programs had value.

I wonder why the volume of useless messages bombarding people coming from the various handheld devices don't bother the general population. Let's face it—dealing with natural disasters is tough enough, but having to maneuver through the inhumane dark side of life, with senseless, constant, in-your-face tweets and films inundated with explicit sex and violents is overpowering and traumatizing.

## Promises coming from the federal level

Too many citizens haven't a clue or don't care that our federal government's and big business's ever-increasing greed continually reaches into every aspect of our society, *unchecked,* thanks to the federal court system. Working for an authoritarian boss or agonizing over crooked politicians can rob you of whatever sanity you have left at the end of the day. We do not need to put up with this! But what can be done? Where do we begin?

## Promises coming from home

Allowing outrageous behaviors to prevail because of broken promises will no longer be tolerated from the government or at home. Instead of shouting vulgar language and ignoring your children, the firm but gentle way, through parental *guidance,* is a far better option and should never be disrespected. Parental guidance is just that, guidance. Don't dwell in the extremes. Dealing only in the black and white areas is not the prudent way to handle problems. There is so much potential when working in the gray areas. Shouting vulgar language and ignoring your kid shows disrespect toward all those involved, whether you participate or observe. One very important facet of respect is to proceed with caution when making promises. If you promise a punishment, say it only once. If the child continues, then carry out the punishment. Keep the punishment between you and your child, do not make a public display of the behavior and punishment. But keep the punishment equal to the misconduct. To repeat the threat of punishment without action can show weakness in your words and deeds and leads the way to negative responses from your kids. For instance, promising a family outing and not following through devastates the kids because they don't understand why you had a change of heart. Start by asking yourself these questions:

- Can I live up to my promises?
- How will these promise's affect others around me?
- Can we hang on as the wind rips through the sails of our ship? Of course we can, provided the whole family is on board. This could be the beginning of world peace! You never know—stranger things have happened.

I could go on and on, but I'll leave other points of view for you to discover. That said, check out the list of books in appendix A9 as well as the books you have on hand.

Notes and dates recorded:

# Chapter 21

Promised liberties forever

The Existing State-of-Affairs or Make It Better for All

Families dedicated to understanding our country's past troubles and triumphs can make today and the future manageable and enjoyable. Why did the United States of America's founders write our precious documents? *To secure everyone's inalienable rights forever!*

In the United States, liberty has lasted for nearly two and a half centuries. To maintain our freedoms for another century or two, let's hoist the sails in the name of liberty. Are you ready to raise the anchor and crew the oars for our voyage up the Potomac? Cue the fireworks!

As a voting citizen in the United States, I am peeved at what my federal government, local government, the US corporations, the pharmaceutical companies, the saturated law industry, and the greedy bankers have done to my liberties. They are assuming that I am willing to give up my inalienable rights. *Not on your life!* For example, I previously mentioned the council majority's proposed landfill site adjacent to the river where 20 percent of our town's drinking water comes from. At a more recent council question-and-answer forum, one councilman kept harping on the reason the project is moving forward: voters in the past two elections said yes to the landfill site. (Methinks the rat I smell is the misinformation the voters were fed.) In fact, the moneyed supporters from the councilman's campaign are behind this project. Fortunately, after an unbiased source made additional facts public, the current voting citizens—armed with accurate knowledge—came forward with a no vote against the landfill location on Election Day. I hoped my fellow voters would remove that *bleep-bleep* politician from office, but he squeaked in. I become a little agitated when people in public office lose their way.

Here is the other side of this little story. I was chosen a few years ago to sit on the Integrated Waste Commission. My fellow commissioners and I went on field trips, listened to speakers in our city council chambers, and even heard concerned citizens who came before our commission. Several little kids presented their renditions of how we could clean up our planet.

Besides being adorable, the kids came up with some impressive solutions. Take that, councilman! My fellow commissioners and I, with the help of a few city employees, were instrumental in educating the public by introducing the Going Zero Waste concept. Things were moving along when, suddenly, the powers that be shut down the commission. Excuse me—the purpose of a citizen's *volunteer* commission is to watch the politicians and city employees and make sure they follow the voters' wishes. The accountability vanished! I don't like the deceitful path my town politicians are taking. Do you have council politicians bullying your town folks?

Speaking of waste, plastic bags are on the way out, and cloth bags are in. However, everyone must wash the cloth bags every week. I pull fabric from my sewing stash to make shopping bags for my neighbors and myself. The cloth bags are stronger and last longer.

US citizens were guaranteed freedoms way back in the 1780s with the ratification of the US Constitution, the Bill of Rights, and many other documents. But what has happened to transparency in government and the idea of citizen representation? Too many elected officials represent the deep pockets of their campaign contributors and completely ignore the voters. Short-circuiting the check-and-balance system of government has hoodwinked voters into accepting the outlandish, money-sucking programs that favor only the wealthy. Dag-nab-bit, I know I'm repeating myself, but are you doing anything about the treasonous actions committed by the people *you* elected to office? And then there are the mega corporations clustering together with career politicians, in private, along with the bankers who are supplying Congress on Capitol Hill with their billions (or trillions or perhaps other sums of money I can't pronounce) of dollars to promote their greedy agendas they exclusively share. Yuck! I just lost a few of my feathers in this one. I'll gather my composure while you continue to read.

The voting citizens of the United States do not want to be controlled by the few greedy heads of industry and banking and misguided politicians. Getting buried in debt is not up for discussion. So far, we have the Constitution and the Bill of Right to back us up.

The banking industry; Washington, DC; and big corporations are less than honest and are way out of line. I suspect these three bodies are *incapable* of understanding why they are out of touch with CEOs' rank-and file employees, DC's constituencies, and big bank executives' small depositors. Every human has wants and needs, as well as at least small degrees of greed. But hang on—people involved up to their eyeballs in excessive greed rob those who know how to control their greedy tendencies. We all live on this planet together. Therefore, taking from people just to guarantee oneself outlandish luxuries must not prevail. Besides, the more you get, the more you want; it's a deadly curse. Do you want to be controlled by a curse? Before we know it, there will be nothing left to take because our country will collapse. Do you want to see that day?

Record numbers of citizens, as well as large numbers of politicians, are no longer accountable for their actions, words, deeds, or worse, self-denial. Looking out for number one and having it all right this minute appears to be the accepted lifestyle. Let me tell you, I'm all for taking care of number one, but not at the expense of others. American voting citizens, we need to recognize the difference between taking care of our families and out-and-out greed. Selfishness in the form of greed is irrational thinking and is leading the country toward an unstable nuclear path. (Is using both *unstable* and *nuclear* in the previous sentence redundant?) Overruling the regular citizens' concerns and doing business with a few campaign supporters could be the root of our nation's money problems. It's *not good!* The possible outcome of such behavior is that without accountability, we have no liberty; and without liberty, we will fall under a dictatorship.

When I say *regular citizens*, I'm referring to the hundreds of thousands of US citizens struggling to pay taxes while receiving a minimum wage. And another thing, CEOs of corporations and bank executives' bribing government officials to write legislation so they won't have to pay their fair share of taxes is *wrong!* I live in San Diego County, where Michael Turko of KUSI Channel 9 is helping us regular citizens level the playing field. His program is called *The Turko Files*, and his catchphrase is, "It ain't fair!" I hope you have someone like Turko fighting in your town.

## Government one-sidedness can't go on

Hundreds of millions of people over the past seven centuries have fled to America to escape total oppression. I don't advocate running away or starting a bloody revolution. But if we *do not* wake up fast and relearn the true meaning of liberty, our country will fall and may never recover. Every citizen with suffrage has a duty in the running of this great country—and shame on those who refuse to register to vote.

We can turn this turmoil around and, in the process, return citizens to a happy and truly free life. Each member of the Family Political Council has the power within his or her grasp. Take on the responsibility so that we all can live lives without tyranny.

Some Americans may think they are living well, but watch out: there are those who are ready to give up their lives to destroy yours.

The Family Political Council is an ongoing endeavor and requires open minds, respect, and compassion from everyone involved. These are learned social skills and will help smooth out most wrongdoings within the family, the neighborhood, the greater community, and so on. Respecting the rules and goals that your council agrees on will give you the clout to empower every citizen in your family to live a truly free life. All citizens have the right to acquire a better understanding of what it is like to live in a healthy society. Remember, do this in the name of democracy and avoid the oppressive frame of mind.

By living a truly free life, anti–American attitudes won't have a chance to develop. So let's all be nice and get to work!

Each family citizen has the duty to be present at all councils. However, if a council member has an opportunity to, say, attend a band retreat when an important vote is pending in your council, voting by proxy can be arranged. This would be an excellent subject to discuss in one of your future councils.

## Personalize your own laws

There are laws to be made, and all family citizens must agree. From the suggested list below, make choices that relate to your council.

1. Interested citizens wishing to speak at the council must request permission from the mayor in writing, *prior to council.*
2. Never interrupt the person speaking. (It's imperative to adopt this one.)
3. No tardiness is accepted unless a trustworthy proof is presented in writing and approved by the mayor. (In an honest world, offering a *trustworthy* proof of tardiness or absence from council is designed to display forward thinking and will help curb excuses for not showing up to council.)
4. All citizens will act in a suitable and professional manner appropriate for council; this can be established by all council citizens using *Robert's Rules of Order* and a book on etiquette.
5. Consider an income-tax session at one of your councils in order to support the children's readiness for the real world.

6. All these entries require forethought and planning, rendering a spur-of-the-moment decision questionable.

7. If a citizen is disrupting council or generally abusing the family laws, he or she will go before the judge, who will hear the facts and pass the appropriate judgment. Any punishment must equal the crime and not be adjudicated beyond the person's ability to pay, but it must be a *little* uncomfortable.

   a. A citizen who wears cut-off jeans to a council is invited to stay while the council is in session but not allowed to speak or vote during that council. Then he or she will go before the judge at a later council.

   b. A citizen who tries to bribe the judge will be subjected to a much harsher punishment, such as forfeiting his or her pay for three months plus relinquishing any voice in council during that time and pulling weeds. In other words, the punishment should be something very undesirable for the offender.

**Rule thirteen:** All citizens must request permission to speak at council meetings in writing a minimum of 2 days in advance!

*It takes less time and effort to do the right thing in the beginning than to exercise deceit.*

A lie will trip you up sooner or later, but honesty will stand up for your cause. If possible, have a witness state in writing the valid reason for your being absent or tardy. This doesn't have to be typed or on formal stationery; a post-it note is acceptable during your probation council period as long as the pertinent info (who, what, where, when, and why) is in plain English, legible, dated, and signed. Transparency carries respect and demonstrates your trustworthiness. The regularity with which an individual chooses selfish thoughts and activities over councils should lessen with time. The downside could be a dishonest person who connives to get away with falsifying legal documents and causing mischief within the ranks. Please don't go there! It's not worth it. These documents are being recorded. Remember, the treasured family teachings, as I mentioned earlier, started the day you are born.

**Rule Fourteen:** Practice the continual presence of politeness and good humor during all councils. These attributes can help diminish less-than productive situations with-in your Family Political Councils.

Okay, I hear you. This sounds too good to be true, but have you tried being honest, willing to go the extra mile, thoughtful, thinking of solutions instead of crying in your beer and so on? You get better results when you practice the virtues mentioned above. Phrases like "You can catch more flies with honey than with vinegar" comes to mind.

Disrupting the family's progress is not to be tolerated. A perpetrator can lose his or her right to vote in two or three councils. Instead, use your words and actions thoughtfully within the established laws. How un–American is it to *not be heard?* In your Family Political Council, there is no path to deportation; that said, following is a list of where lawbreakers could do their time:

- family—their bedroom or "the dog house"
- neighborhood—house arrest
- community—barred from your favorite community activities

While observing a city council meeting, I became painfully aware of one reason governing bodies have devastated the US economy during the first two decades of the twenty-first century. Issues are left *unfinished!* Every day my city government is faced with stiff fines due to postponing repairs or replacements of old water and sewage pipes. A few years back, a pipe burst at the cliff overlooking a small, picturesque residential community on the beach in my town. What a mess. A fellow commissioner and I observed the damage firsthand just hours after the break. This time, the council and city staff could not deny where, when, or how much damage was created. The two of us were viable witnesses. Time is money, in this case to the tune of hundreds of thousands of dollars for every day the pipes were not fixed. Maybe the city council citizens were turning their backs on all the facts. Maybe these fines should come out of their pay. I don't know how you feel, but I'm tired of taking it on the chin (and emptying out my coin purse) due to the city councilmembers' short-sightedness.

Personal thoughts from my research:

In Bill O'Reilly's book *The O'Reilly Factor,* in the chapter entitled "The Money Factor," he states on page 17, "This country (United States) has developed a ridiculous blind spot: the power and glorification of money." On the next page, he writes, "The working people of the U.S. are the most important ingredient in the enduring American

Story." My purpose for writing *Keep Voting, America* is to reach several segments of our population and encourage them to form their own Family Political Councils. Maybe then the working folks can once again lead our country toward a peaceful and productive society for all Americans wanting to strive for a better quality of life and not just more of the stuff that commerce wants us to buy. Explain to me why you want an overabundance of money.

Space is provided below. Be careful what you wish for!

Why do you want the big bucks?

Your list appears to be a little excessive, don't cha think?

# CHAPTER 22

Let's talk taxes. It might hurt, so....

I was going to say "man up" but decided to omit this cliché because (1) many people are confused as to what message the cliché conveys; (2) the sheer redundancy of a cliché often renders empty meanings; (3) single words and cut-off phrases uttered without any regard for the audience, in addition to the rest of the unthinking population repeating willy-nilly these empty words and phrases, soon become inappropriate, ill-informed, unwanted, and useless jargon. Therefore, I'm going to start over and proceed with ameliorated words.

## Let's talk taxes. I'll share a few facts with you!

There, isn't this better? Now I have included everyone—women, men, boys, and girls!

I know most citizens feel they are taxed unfairly. But for those of us needing clarification, let's examine the following table. (Please don't kill the messenger if the figures are not quite accurate. My aim is to approximate figures.)

| Taxpayer | Yearly Income | How Income Is Generated | If Taxed at ... | Amt. Deducted from Paycheck |
|----------|---------------|-------------------------|-----------------|------------------------------|
| Mary | $100,000 | Wages | 1% | $1,000 |
| Linda | $130,000 | Self-employed | 24% | $31,000 |
| Note: Both taxpayers have "earned income," which is basically wages from a job. | | | | |

Sounds just about right, yes? Let's look a little closer and introduce a third person, Joe.

- Of Mary's $100,000 in wages, $70,000 is subjected to a 50 percent income tax, which equals $35,000. Added to the $1,000 of tax deducted earlier, her total tax is $4,500.

- In addition to the $31,000 in FICA deductions, Linda must pay a 4 percent state and city income tax, bringing her total tax burden to $36,000.
- Our newcomer, Joe, inherited $500,000 per year. (This is "unearned income," money from interest, capital gains, pension, stock market, or a large inheritance). His tax payment is zero dollars. How can this be?

Per the Constitution, Joe should be paying 5 percent in FICA deductions ($25,000) as well as a 25 percent income tax ($125,000), for a total of $150,000.

Could *you* live on $350,000 a year? I certainly would make the sacrifice! Up front I would hire a veteran to be my chauffeur and pay her a handsome salary to drive my Ford Escort.

After close inspection, when it comes to tax laws, it appears the earned income folks are not getting representation from Congress. Does this indicate taxation without representation? What do you think?

## Manufacturing and service industries are hiring employees, hopefully!

Today the service industry is reaching 90 percent of the gross national product (GNP). But these three letters puzzle me. A *service,* when offered, is not an *item* made from raw material or recycled items. A product manufactured from raw materials, such as a tree, is processed in someone's garage or a furniture factory into something the consumer can purchase, like a chair. In the olden days, housewives cut up worn-out clothes and made quilts.

On the other hand, today's service industry offers an ever-growing assortment of services to purchase from providers such as a dentist, the waitress at a restaurant, private school teachers, cable television line workers, the court stenographer, the ever-popular dating web sites, the water taxi in the marina, and so on. In our free economy, the sale of products creates profits, whereas services create wealth.

## A familiar conversation —

Citizen A: "There is a cliché circulating around town: the love of money is the root of all evil!"
Citizen B: "So?"
Citizen A: "Money doesn't motivate me. I volunteer as often as I can."
Citizen B: "Does volunteering pay the rent?"

Citizen A: "No! But what kind of a life is it when you worry that the baddies of the world can hack your credit card?"

Citizen B: "Oh, yeah. My neighbor's credit card info was lifted at Target."

Citizen A: "How can money rule everything you do in life when something like that happens so close to home?"

Citizen B: "Good question!"

Notes and dates recorded:

# UNIT THREE

# CHAPTER 23

## What's yet to come in your council

*Suggestions to keep up the momentum for future councils*

With the presence of children in your council, you might start with the school district governing body:

- Who are the school board officials? Everyday people? Teachers?
- Is there a state school board?
- What decisions are these board members making?
- Why do we need a school board governing district?
- Did you know that the school board meetings are open to the rank and file?
- How often do they meet?
- Is there a term limit to sit on the school board?

## Providing children with a running start to adulthood

Following are a few suggested ways that each Family Political Council can prepare children for a smooth entry into adulthood. Note the school years for each lesson.

| Age 2–18 | Teach kids the ins and outs of TV ads. Be firm but gentle. |
|---|---|
| 1st–12th | Volunteer for Meals on Wheels, Habitat for Humanity, and so on. |
| 5th–12th | Write letters in longhand to congress. (using your special letterhead stationary) |
| 6th–12th | Do minor repairs in the home. |
| 8th–12th | Invite an income-tax preparer to give a workshop on a simple tax form (twenty minutes). |
| 9th–12th | Investigate watering system contractors or solar panel companies. |
| 12th grade | Visit a school board meeting if approved; take your journal. |

This is a further explanation of the above chart:

- Teach kids how they can avoid the devious messages and not fall for the "buy me" spiel.
- Make sure the volunteer organization is legitimate.
- Handwritten letters to Congress indicate that you have considered the issue carefully. Address one issue at a time so you don't overload the bureaucrats.
- As parents, make sure you set aside time to *oversee* the repairperson's efforts. Leave the electrical, plumbing, and roofing to the experts. If you get approval, by all means observe the professionals. Remember to check their licenses before you hire them. All family members have a stake in projects concerning your house; therefore, debate and then vote on the project and the necessary money (budget) to get the job done.
- Knowledge on income taxes can be helpful for teenagers getting ready to enter the workforce. You do know that animal control officers get a salary while in office, yes? Tell the tax preparer to make instruction simple.
- You might plan a small landscape project or install solar panels.
- Observing your local school board will give the students and you, the parents, a better understanding of how the school works.

Use your imagination when setting up your projects, and have fun with your Family Political Council.

## A big fat piggy bank

In my reference to children receiving a salary while in office (in the form of deposits to a savings account), think of it as a child's first piggy bank. I thank Bill O'Reilly for this wonderful image. Your son or daughter can watch the money grow as they grow. Come graduation day, the children will appreciate how they and their nest egg has matured, and they will have a much more powerful rite of passage when it comes to the choices they make on "payday." Write legislation regarding the legal ownership of this piggy bank savings account, but keep the language understandable for your kids. One scenario is that graduates may choose to purchase a car, in which case you might enlighten them on the facts about the precious automobile for which they just forked over a bunch of money for the sole purpose of joyriding around town. The car's value drops *significantly* due to depreciation the moment the tires roll off the sales lot. Oops! There goes the budget. I hope they saved some money for gas.

The sky's the limit from here on out. Who knows? Maybe your son, daughter, or even you might consider running for mayor, county assessor, attorney general, or—dare I say—president of the United States of America.

You know the drill—notes and dates recorded:

# CHAPTER 24

## Career politicians make extremely poor listeners

When employees continue to demonstrate poor work habits or don't listen to the boss, they can be fired. It appears our career politicians demonstrate poor listening habits as they continue to pass legislation the citizens have plainly voiced that they do not want. Voting citizens have grounds for sacking the rogue office holders by voting them out of office. We have the right.

In your council, discuss the term of office and the number of terms a citizen can hold that office. This way, all interested citizens have an opportunity to run for office. Any office! All offices! Every office! Each office! Also discuss a much lower cost for campaigning. Millions of dollars are way too much.

The original intent was for the political office holder to be temporary, not a career. Back in the nineteenth century, a regular citizen like Gordon farming his land or Mary making her hats or Oscar the sundry store owner could run for public office. When his or her term of office was complete, the former politician returned to plowing his fields, making her hats, or selling his wares.

As I write this book, the mayor of San Diego has resigned, finally. He got too comfortable in his surroundings and overstepped his boundaries. The phrase "familiarity breeds contempt" comes to mind. The public is speaking out. Politicians who feel they are above the law, beware; it's a new day with new accountability! A politician's time in the public service arena—say, the mayor—is approximately two terms. After his or her term is up and the unemployed politician wants to continue in public service, she or he can run for another political position, such as US senator. This is democracy in action.

## A two party system—

Today, several groups are carving out their own parties, like the Green Party and the Libertarian Party. Who said we must be a two-party government?

It's interesting to note that the Libertarian Party is recognized in thirty-seven states and the Green Party in twenty-two states. (These figures may be outdated by the time the book gets published.) There are many more parties; the list is long. The states of Florida, Mississippi, and South Carolina recognize ten parties each. *Wow!* How can the citizens keep up?

You should discuss the political positions, duration, salary, and so on and craft laws after you decide to continue your once-a-week, go-unplugged Family Political Council.

## Welfare

The concept of welfare came from European attempts to create a temporary means of economic support. Here in America, the government set up the welfare system during the Depression era so that massive numbers of unemployed citizens could put food on the table and maintain a house to place that table in. The government tried to stem the tide of this newly impoverished class of citizens by issuing other personal items in the form of household goods as a means of support until the family could secure a living wage in good faith. It was commonly known as a hand up. Where did our government in the 1930s get the "money" for these generous offerings?

That was the plan then, but through the decades welfare grew to such a degree that the recipients became totally dependent on it for life, and now it's a handout. Our Constitution does *not* guarantee federal or local funding to finance American families for *life*. Where did this notion come from? Did it just evolve? I should think you would like some answers.

Many welfare families have a profusion of time on their hands, as well as the potential to discover our rich history and become champions of truth and justice by making the effort to talk with one another in their unique Family Political Councils. The same goes for families in which Mom or Pop is doing time in prison and the siblings visit them.

## Social Security Taxes (FICA)

Just before the turn of the nineteenth century, the new working class of people—the factory workers—received a minuscule salary or company script. The possibility of retiring after a lifetime of labor was unheard of back then. Many young families were compelled to make room in their modest homes for their parents who were determined unfit to work. In one way, this was a good thing because the elders could help with home chores and babysitting. Life had become extremely difficult for the working folks until midway through the Great Depression, when President Roosevelt had the foresight to come up with several plans to help the economy recover. At first this plan showed no merit. This is how the New Deal played out: the working-class employees had a percentage of their pay withheld from their wages, and then after the employees retired, they would receive a benefit of money each month until death. In the beginning, strong opposition from both employees and employers threatened the success of this New Deal program called Social Security.

Later, everyone's attitudes changed when citizens started to collect their due in the form of social security monthly payments. The creators named the paycheck deductions a social security tax. The idea was kind of a platform for a savings account. The workers contributed to their retirement instead of frittering away all their hard-earned cash. The second side of this coin was in the form of employers' matching the employees' deducted amount and placing this money in a social security tax fund provided for under the Federal Insurance Contribution Act, or FICA. This way, the employees would have a modest retirement nest egg, and the employers could hold onto loyal workers—a mutual admiration society, if you will. The help was no longer a handout; instead, it was a hand up! I remember the day I accepted my first job and applied for my first social security card. I was thrilled to be joining society as a valued, independent citizen and earning my own way. The other half of this value came when I stepped into the voting booth and made my mark. Gosh, I was a valuable voting citizen, making my own way, and satisfied that I was being counted on Election Day. I still have my original paper card. After fifty-plus years, my card is dog-eared and faded a bit. Laminated cards had not yet been invented.

Right-of-passage into the world of independence --

Heck, today, social security numbers are given to infants. It saddens me to know that today's children, as they grow into adulthood, will never experience the joy, benefit, and satisfaction as they enter the job market and experience that first rite of passage into the world of independence. Maybe this is too simplistic for today's youth, or maybe the youth automatically have a sense of entitlement because they were born after 1990. Who changed the rules? Children don't have paying jobs, so what wages are being withheld? After talking with a neighbor about this subject, I came to recognize the motive for the change. Her explanation for the assigning of a social security number to a newborn child was so that the practice of falsifying the number of dependents on income tax forms would stop. I wonder why the powers that be didn't come up with a different source for the proof of family dependents. Looks like the politicians aren't the only ones in town denying transparency.

During the past decade, we have been told that social security retirement funds are nearly gone. *Grrrr!*

- Where did my social security money go?
- Who "borrowed" it?
- Is the money going to be paid back? When?
- Are there promissory notes?
- Who is holding these promissory notes?
- All the presidents and congress people who borrowed from my social security tax fund should be forced to pay back every red cent they took. And do not allow them to borrow the money; the right thing for them to do is to pay back the money out of their personal coffers. Oh, and they should send me an apology letter and proof of payment in full for their transgressions. No postdated checks!
- *And*, for all the people willing to defraud the government by faking an incapacitating injury, either come clean or leave my country. Sorry—that's another kettle of smelly fish to discuss. Maybe later.

## American society's vast array of voters

Following are examples of several human components making up the collective American citizenry with suffrage (registered voters):

- family: mother, father, children over the voting age
- neighbors: the couple next door, Aunt Mary on Hill Street, the Jones family around the corner, and their two children in college
- community: Ed's coffee and donut shop employees, Councilwoman Gardner and her family, Officer Blair and his wife, the janitor at the local high school, and actors at the community theater
- city: the mayor and his wife, the city manager and her husband, and city street cleaners and their families
- county: school board administrators, courtroom employees, and the county assessor and his family
- state: your grandparents upstate, John who owns John's Tree Distribution Service and his family, and the governor and his wife
- federal: US congress people, FBI personnel, the federal judge and her family, the president and his wife, and IRS investigators

Registered voters maintain their status as US voters when they take a proactive approach to governing this country. It is a simple idea, voting; however, the unchecked powers that be are mucking up the process so that many voters have a hard time understanding what they are voting for. Even worse, some voters are blocked from getting to the voting places. Talk in your Family Political Council and discover what you can do to ensure our constitutional right to register and vote.

Everyday people, from the family to the national government, have certain attachments:

- People are more attached to their families than their neighbors.
- They are more attached to their neighbors than to the community at large.
- City employees work well, or not, with other city employees in their department.
- People of each state feel a bias toward the state government rather than toward the government of the United States.
- Residents of Washington, DC have the federal government in their front yards, making it a huge part of their daily lives.

We humans tend to cluster in harmonious groups, but then our toes get stepped on when legislation favors demands coming from other cliques before ours has had a chance to be heard. All too often, more than toes get bruised. We intuitively know there are all sorts of isolating factors, like ethnicity, religion, meat eaters, stay-at-home moms or dads, and those people toting guns living just down the street. How are we to get along with so much diversity? Good question! Maybe we can find it in our Constitution.

**Rule fifteen:** Carry on using the spirit of goodwill!

Our Constitution was ratified around two hundred and fifty years ago, prompting us to strive toward "a more perfect union." The family citizens must be knowledgeable about our political history as well as what is happening in politics today; please include children under the voting age. Don't just learn dates and battlefields. Walk in the footsteps of people who campaigned for public office in the early 1900s. Also, we all need to examine how the political voting districts are defined.

Have you joined throngs of citizens walking up Pennsylvania Avenue in our nation's capital and knew for certain that your discontent was heard and understood? Or maybe you demonstrated on the steps of your city hall? I did, and we definitely were heard. Remember, we must be vigilant and persistent in our actions. Get used to being truthful on a daily basis and do it in the *spirit of* goodwill. Remember, anything (make sure it is legal) new and worthwhile is awkward at first but unquestionably the bottom line: your efforts will be validated!  Do not pay much attention to the ridiculous TV ads and the barrage of campaign propaganda in your mailbox. Dig deeper to find the facts.

Goodwill is something many business owners *toil* (see, even the boss is a laborer) diligently for as they extend helpful, courteous, and friendly service toward their customers. Employees can claim "ownership" of customers as well, mainly because the employees work closely with the customers. Well-trained employees have the willingness to go the extra mile for their employers and their customers. When the exchange of goods and services is completed in a pleasurable and satisfying way, we now have a valuable commodity called *goodwill*. Repeated patronage of the establishment continues, and the business owner's goodwill increases. The boss gets richer, the employees can now send their kids to college, and the customers know they will be treated with respect and come home with the highest quality products for their dollars spent. At least this was the scenario a century ago. Today, shoppers want to spend the least amount possible. Sadly, the product is so poorly made that we are compelled to spend more money much too soon to replace the worn-out item. It's not much of a bargain if you ask me! The same goes for services. One day, I hired the next-to-lowest bidder for a carpentry project in my home. Well, the guy left in the middle of the home improvement job, leaving me with a total mess. And the guy had a valid contractor's license! What happens to people when they get the taste of money?

Notes and dates recorded:

# CHAPTER 25

## Putting America to work

Big government and corporate America create jobs. This is good—I think. Let's take a closer look at the jobs they create. Below are samples of jobs within selected industries and one undesirable duty for each job.

Hotel

| | |
|---|---|
| Maid | Cleans toilets |
| Desk clerk | Deals with irate guests |
| Night manager | Handles truant employees |
| CEO | Reports to stockholders when the bottom line drops, oops |

Manufacturing

| | |
|---|---|
| Assembly line | Repeats same task all day long |
| Product expediter | Runs forklift that is not functioning as expected |
| Salesperson | Travels a lot, leaving little if any time for family |
| CEO | Has nothing to do—oh, well! |

Restaurants

| | |
|---|---|
| Busboy | Takes out mounds of trash |
| Waitress | Carries heavy trays of food |
| Manager | Continually changes employee work schedules |
| Chef | Catches favorite employee stealing bottles of wine—what to do? |

City employees

| | |
|---|---|
| Park custodian | Cleans toilets |
| Water dept. clerk | Deals with irate customers |
| Librarian | Finds books with page corners dog-eared and stains on pages |
| City manager | loosing endorsement from the councilmembers |

Bank employees

| Clerk or teller | Has too many bosses to answer to |
| --- | --- |
| Custodian | Cleans toilets |
| Loan officer | Places his or her reputation on the line |
| Bank manager | Confesses to the shareholders when loans go into default, dang |

Construction employees

| Hog | Carries concrete to bricklayers |
| --- | --- |
| Office worker | shredding endless papers. |
| On-site foreman | Deals with non-English speaking laborers |
| Company owner | Is summoned to court, ouch! |

## More ideas to ponder

- What happened to transparency in government?
- Why are we not holding these public servants accountable?
- Why do we encourage legislators to fix whatever the country needs fixing without any guidance from the voting public in the form of volunteer citizen commission boards?
- Why are we giving up our rights? Regretfully, that is exactly what we are doing!
- Could it be that we have too many federal government employees?
- The corporation was created right here in the United States, and the Supreme Court made the corporation a legal person. I beg your pardon!
- How many politicians are well-off financially? Every politician gets a salary. What would happen if the wealthy public office holders donated half of their salaries to programs like Meals on Wheels or a maintenance program for the book mobile? Make sure the politicians' efforts secure fresh, healthy food for the Meals on Wheels program and keep the book mobile gassed up and ready for its rounds.
- The political campaign people are getting away with artificially carving up the land into election districts for the sole purpose of guaranteeing the vote for their candidates. Talk about the lack of transparency and even betrayal aimed directly at the voting public!
- Why are political appointees passing laws when the citizens are clearly voicing displeasure? Perhaps voters are going about this whole thing in the wrong way.

- How many citizens are needed to march up Pennsylvania Avenue to be heard?
- Why has the "political elite" (family business) become so powerful that they feel the citizens (US voters) owe them job security? I'm cringing on this one!
- Did you know CEO's have no real power in their corporations? I know it's hard to believe.
- Are the political appointees reading the personal letters and e-mails we send to them?
- Are the politicians working on our behalf? We elected them to do so!
- Why is the federal government tapping into our personal phone calls and e-mails? I know I'm not a threat to our country. Are you? (You are? Shame on you!)
- Do you believe the public servants in Washington, DC (as they write legislation) picture your face or the faces of those who richly contributed to their campaigns? The same can be asked of CEOs. Do they picture the faces of their employees who work hard to make the best toothpicks or the faces of their shareholders?
- The corporations are wickedly clever; they can find loopholes annexing the laws governing campaign contributions. Clever individuals can grease the right joints to quiet the squeaks and not break one law in the process. What goes wrong with people once they gain wealth and fame? The potential to get ugly didn't happen when my fellow retirees convinced enough voters to vote down Prop E. We won by a two-thirds majority because us old folks were clever enough to *follow the money* and stick to our commitments.

Notes and dates recorded:

# CHAPTER 26

## Returning to a free society

Let's set an even keel and sail our political ship away from foul weather!

Every US citizen with suffrage has the power to correct the calamities ravaging our country, but remember to save a little time and effort so you can pay attention to your family's issues. Following is a list of activities; include all council citizens when checking each one off as the task is completed.

- Establish a Family Political Council in order to solve any family glitches, and then take time to learn the US Constitution and how it affects every citizen daily.
- Visit city council meetings when you can; shop, play, and do business with local merchants and the mom-and-pop businesses within your county or township.
- Gather your children together and take a couple of hours a month to volunteer. *
- Take a drive to the state capitol and observe the elected public servants in action. Before the visit, be sure you do some reading about the subjects that the legislators will be talking about that day so that you will better understand the process.
- Take time to observe the vote count after the election. Did you know that regular citizens with suffrage can do this? Contact your local voter registration office for more information.
- Maybe allow yourself to feel good about paying your fair share of federal income tax.
- Above all, let's have fun and *play nice!* In other words, do not get into the attitude "I know it all and I alone can change things."

*A short list of non-profit groups to volunteer for:

- Bay Area Children's Theatre
- Yuma Community Food Bank
- Special Olympics Wyoming
- HandsOn Kansas State
- Oceanside, CA Visitors Center
- Vintage Shop in your neighborhood
- American Red Cross in South Carolina

This is a strenuous agenda, but as the saying goes, take baby steps at first. As your council develops, you will find your courage growing, making you a full-fledged patriot. What a joyous and satisfying quality of life your family will experience through positive involvement in US government—at all levels!


Notes and dates recorded:

# CHAPTER 27

Here's a list of worthwhile habits to develop in order to be a patriot in US society. How many of these ideals do you follow?

- demonstrating love of country: Keep it real, and don't go overboard or you may drown.
- voting: "At the most basic level, we do so by voting with our feet as we remain here in this country rather than living elsewhere." This one's a given *if* you are legal to be here!
- obeying the laws
- flying the US flag in front of your house: As a safety precaution, I placed an American flag on my tricycle pole to let car drivers know I'm sharing the road with them. Every once in a while, a motorist (probably a vet) will honk his horn and wave as he passes me. *
- registering to vote and then making your mark at every election: When voters choose not to vote in the primary and special elections, they are missing the boat. Check online: The year of low turnout and the consequences of not voting – to see how elections affect us adversely when registered citizens don't vote.
- being honest and forthright
- making sure the elected politicians stay accountable through volunteer citizen commissions
- activating your own Family Political Council

*Update: September 30, 2017: as I was riding my tricycle across the busy street on my way home from Curves, I heard the familiar sound of a horn. This time the driver was a woman: she even gave me a thumbs-up!

## Where tattered and faded American flags go

Did you know that the act of throwing an American flag in the garbage is disrespectful? According to the US Flag Code, burning is the right thing to do to your tattered and faded US flag. According to *RealSimple* magazine (July 2013, p. 38), "When done ceremoniously and in private, rather than in protest, setting fire to the flag isn't a sacrilege. Worried about safety? Make America and your local fire marshal proud by dropping off your tattered and faded Stars and Stripes at the nearest American Legion office. Its members are pleased to incinerate it for you. Find the one closest to you online at http://www.legion.org. Also, you could call the Girl Scout headquarters to see if a troop is currently learning how to dispose of the US flag.

Becoming a family of community-minded citizens through the United States Family Liberty Plan is an honest enterprise, this is just one definition of filling the shoes of a US patriot. I hope you give *Keep Voting, America* plan serious thought. By doing so, you support the ideal for working toward a more perfect union. A patriot is *not* defined by how much money and stuff you own. A patriot facilitates the running of this great country and steps up to defend our way of life—period!

When we participate in the political process, we make sure our elected trustees are working for us. Americans generate the assurance that every voting citizen has quality of life. One way we can empower the voting citizen is by initiating the United States Family Liberty Plan. All Family Political Council citizens across the United States have the right to demonstrate using soft power, proving to Washington, DC that we possess the steadfastness of patriotism and are ready to reclaim our inalienable rights. But start at your local level first. Can do? I knew you had it in you! Keep this in mind: contrary to popular opinion, *politics* is not a four-letter word but a tried-and-true way of guiding US citizens toward harmonious lives.

America truly is a melting pot. For example, I live in California in a fifty-five and older community where the residents live in affordable housing: our community is not part of Section 8. Instead, we pay for rent control. There are so many folks living here representing different countries that I have lost count. Half of my extended neighbors own their homes. I own my house, receive social security, and live a reasonably comfortable life. I can't say this will continue if my town suffers a sudden natural disaster, as I live in earthquake country. For now, the neighborhood is quiet and safe. Most of my extended neighbors are retirees, and others are still chasing the paycheck. In the fourteen-plus years I have lived here, there has been only one car crash, and wouldn't you know it was right in front of my house. The only emergency vehicles driving through my neighborhood are fire and aid trucks; you should see the huge hook-and-ladder truck maneuvering through our narrow streets. Amazing! We did lose one home to fire last year. I was sad when I heard the folks decided not to rebuild.

My neighbor across the street rents her house. Hers is larger than mine and much newer. We have meaningful conversations from time to time. She is a teaching chef.

I only mention this because she harvests figs from my huge fig tree and makes the best Figgie Jam, of which I get a couple of jars each season. She doesn't own a car as she prefers to rent one when traveling to her teaching jobs about every other month. She travels by air to other states and even countries.

Another close neighbor turned one hundred years old in 2017. She has lots of interesting stories to tell, and she loves to talk politics, much to my liking.

I pretty much stay at home. I have no budget to travel farther than my local community, where nearly every need I have is a tricycle ride away. Several of us ride trikes, some ride bikes, and many more drive cars. I pedal my trike to the stores and even to Curves, extending my daily exercise routine. I have two baskets and use them to bring home plenty of cargo, mostly groceries and dry cleaning. On occasion, I bring home a thrift shop find.

People of different ethnic backgrounds, languages, lifestyles, work histories, ages, income levels—many slices of diversity—live in my neighborhood. And we all get along well, waving to one another, stopping to chat a while, offering rides to those without transportation, and simply living in a pleasant environment.

Just before the last election, I was asked to help several neighbors better understand the confusing voting ballot. This was to be their first time to vote in America because they had recently completed the naturalization process. I get smiles to this day due to my paying it forward; you see, I registered many of my neighbors for the vote.

I'm now finished writing this book. But first, I would like to thank Bill O'Reilly for these words of wisdom: "We're all born with a grab bag of gifts and gaps." I will paraphrase his take on the *lack of discipline:* A cure for the lack of discipline is to learn to make yourself do what you *need* to do, get it done on time and then do what you *want* to do.

My question to you is this: What keeps you from identifying your talents and using them? Tomorrow is going to be a better day once your Family Political Council is up and running!

Notes and dates recorded:

# UNIT FOUR

# APPENDICES

{IMAGE|}
Picture an old wooden ballot box with rope handles sitting at the end of the voters' sign-in table.

# Appendix A1

## Political Offices of the Federal and State Governments, 1925

This is dry reading, so just take a quick look. The next two pages are meant to be a guide for your Family Political Council office holders.

| Source of Power | US Constitution | Individual State Constitution |
|---|---|---|
| Legislative Branch | Congress: Senate; House | Legislature: same qualifications as senator |
| | 1. Be 30 years of age and older | 1. Be citizen of US |
| | 2. Citizen of US for nine years | 2. Not criminal or pauper |
| | 3. Resident of state where chosen and elected... | 3. Elected by people |
| | Qualifications for Representative | |
| | 1. At least 25 years old | |
| | 2. Citizen of US for 7 years | |
| | 3. Resident of state where chosen | |
| | 4. May not be an officer of the US | |
| | 5. May be a "delegate'" from a territory | |
| Executive Branch | The President and Council | The Governor, administrative |
| | The Secretary of State | The Secretary of State |
| | The Secretary of Treasury | The State Treasurer |
| | The Attorney General | The State Auditor |
| | The Postmaster General | The Attorney General |
| | The Secretary of the Navy | The Superintendent of Public Instruction |
| | The Secretary of the Interior | Commissioners: |

| | | |
|---|---|---|
| | The Secretary of Agriculture | Insurance |
| | The Secretary of Commerce and Labor | Integrated Waste |
| | Commissioners: | Board of Agriculture |
| | The Interstate Commerce | |
| | The Civil Service | |
| | The Fish and Game | |
| | The Labor | |
| | The Weather Bureau | |
| | The Librarian of Congress | |
| | The Government Printing Office | |
| | Foreign Ambassador, Ministers and Consuls | |
| Judicial Branch | Supreme Court: | Supreme Court: |
| | Chief Justice + 8 associates | Chief Justice + 7 associates |

I told you this would be boring.

# Appendix A2

## City and County Governments, 1925

The Mayor: Term one to four years. Presides at council. Functions partly administrative, partly legislative. Duties mainly executive or appointive.

The Common Council: Usually one body called aldermen. Two from each ward (district), one elected every other year. Must live in ward. Term is one to four years. Duties are mainly to pass ordinances for the city's government and to control city finances.

The Officers: There is no uniform rule as to election or number. Usually the mayor, council citizens, and the heads of certain important departments are elective; the remaining officials get their offices by appointment. Duties: Primarily, the mayor, council, and the other officers are expected to unite in having the city accomplish its purpose as a part of local government. The administration of justice, the assessment of equalization of taxes, the improvement and protection of property, the *care of public morals,* the promotion of civic interest, the welfare of the schools—these and many other matters in the city are dependent upon faithful officials.

County Government (The county seat)

The officers include the county board: Composed of three to seven commissioners or supervisors, elected by the people, and with corporate powers.
The County Auditor is the secretary of the board and keeps the county accounts, tax lists, and valuable papers.
The County Treasurer is the guardian of the public's money, financial agent, and collector.
The County Superintendent of Schools usually licenses teachers and has oversight of the schools.
The County Surveyor determines property boundaries.
The County Attorney attends to the county's legal matters.
The County Sheriff keeps the peace.
The Clerk of the Court records court proceedings.
The County Commissioner acts in the absence of a judge.

Oath and Pay: Every official is required to take an oath to perform his or her duties. Compensation is determined by the County Board.

(From the Standard Reference Work Vol. X, Chicago Standard Education Society, 1925, out of print. A friend I frequently accompanied to city hall for council meetings graciously gave me this book, Thanks Jimmy.)

# Appendix A3

## Your Family's Voter Sign-In Book and Ballot

Following is a sample entry in your family's sign-in book on Election Day.

| Date of election | Citizen's name | Voter's signature | Address | City | State |
|---|---|---|---|---|---|
| 6/5/14 | John Harris | | 123 A Street | Any Town | Any state |

## Sample of Ballot on Sticky Note

If you have the time and the know-how, you might create a pamphlet to look like the real one.

| November 14, 2014 Election |
|---|
| Mayor:     Jane Doe     ☐ |
| Mother     ☐ |
| Write-in     ☐ |

Appendix A4

Congressional District Maps

Check out these congressional maps. How convoluted can these districts get?

This is the result of gerrymandering the voting districts. Observe the disjointed districts. Talk about hoodwinking the public. Could it be caused by unadulterated greed? Or maybe it's the lack of transparency? Rigging the election districts without voter input? I think all the above. It is amazing yet out-and-out flabbergasting.

Gerrymandered districts have shapes that are akin to that of a salamander.

# Appendix A5

## Two Versions of the Naturalization Process for Becoming a US Citizen

### Version One, 1925

In 1925, when a legal alien wished to become a US citizen, he or she needed to go through the following steps:

1. Go before a US district court in the district where the person lives and declare intention in writing to become a citizen of the United States. This can be done any time after the alien turns eighteen years old and must contain the following,
    a. Name in full
    b. Age and occupation
    c. Time and place of arrival in the United States
    d. The declarant's intention to become a *bona fide* citizen of the United States and to renounce all allegiance and fidelity to any foreign country or principality, and at that time become a citizen or subject.
2. In order to file a petition, a person must wait a minimum of two years after the initial declaration. He or she must have continuous residence in the United States for five years prior to the declaration. And immediately prior to filing, the person must have resided for a minimum of one year continuously in any court district. The petition should be signed in the candidate's own handwriting and contain:
    a. name in full
    b. complete address: street number and name, city, county, and state
    c. occupation
    d. birth date and last foreign place lived
    e. place from which person embarked for the United States and the date, name of ship, the line to which it belongs, date and place of arrival in the United States
    f. height, weight, and so on at the time; occupation
    g. the names of those who came with the petitioner and the name of the place they were going to
    h. when and where the declaration of intent was taken
    i. all information on each family member must be given:

- names
- date and place of birth
- state where they live now
- state and country they belong to
- when residence began in the United States
- state in which petition is offered or previous petition made for US citizenship (if so, date and place and cause of refusal)

When petition is filed, it must be verified by affidavits of two credible witnesses who are citizens of the United States.

These witnesses must declare under oath that:

1. They have known the petitioner during his or her entire residence where the petition is filed.
2. They know the petitioner has resided there not less than one year immediately preceding the filing of the petition.
3. They have known the petitioner to be a resident of the United States continuously during the five years immediately preceding the filing of petition.
4. Petitioner has acted as a person of good moral character.
5. Petitioner is attached to the principles of the Constitution of the United States and well disposed toward the good order and happiness of the same.

The court will then issue a Petition of Naturalization for which the petitioner pays four dollars. In not less than ninety days after issuing the Petition for Naturalization and not less than thirty days before a general election, the petitioner may be notified by the court to appear for examination. He or she should be accompanied by the witnesses whose affidavits were filed with the petition. The petitioner will be examined in open court on his or her knowledge of the Constitution of the United States, knowledge of the government of the state and city or town in which he or she resides, and ability to read and write the English language.

If this examination is satisfactory, a Certificate of Naturalization is issued and the alien becomes an American citizen. Yeah!

The following classes of persons are denied naturalization (1925 list):

1. Chinese, Japanese, Koreans, and Hindus
2. persons opposed to the Constitution of the United States
3. anarchists

4. criminals
5. polygamists
6. persons belonging to any organization or association that teaches disbelief in organized government
7. persons of questionable moral character
8. persons not correctly informed about the government of the United States

These books may be helpful for teachers or anyone else who would like more information on citizenship and how the process has evolved:

- *An Outline Course in Citizenship*, Bulletin 1919, Number 76, Bureau of Naturalization, Washington, DC
- *Use Your Government*, Alisa Franc
- *The New Voter*, Thompson
- *Government and Politics in U.S.*, Gateau

Subject material was taken from *The Standard Reference Work for the Home, School, and Library*, Vol. X, Chicago: Standard Education Society USA, 1925. Out of print.

## Version Two, 2010

In less than a hundred years, the fee has jumped to over seven hundred dollars, but the information is easier to retrieve since it is on the Internet. I did not read the entire application; therefore, I did not see if the applicant still had to give the name of the ship and the line on which he or she traveled to the United States. It is quite time consuming and cumbersome to go into the entire procedure. I will quote the official Oath of Allegiance:

> I hereby declare, on oath; that I absolutely and entirely renounce and abjure all allegiance and fidelity to any foreign prince, potentate, state, or sovereignty, of whom or which I have heretofore been a subject or citizen; that I will support and defend the Constitution and laws of the United States of America against all enemies, foreign and domestic; that I will bear true faith and allegiance to the same; that I will bear arms on behalf of the United States when required by the law; that I will perform non-combatant service in the Armed Forces of the United States when required by the law; that I will perform work of national importance under civilian direction when required by law; and that I take this

obligation freely without any mental reservation or purpose of evasion; so help me God.

Let's define a few of the words for clarity:

| | | |
|---|---|---|
| *potentate:* monarch, ruler | *fidelity:* devotion | *allegiance:* loyalty |
| *renounce:* give up | *sovereignty:* power | *work of national importance:* serve on a jury |
| *evasion:* shirking | *bear arms:* go to war | |

Note that there is no mention of following a moral and civil code within our neighborhoods, greater communities, states, or national societies. There is no mention of working in harmony alongside other citizens of the United States and no mention of the freedoms we hold so dear.

At the time I started writing this book (2010), the immigration department was not accepting any applications for citizenship because of the horrifyingly destructive terrorist attack on September 11, 2001.

Appendix A6

A Brief Notation from *Robert's Rules of Order,* 10th ed., Newly Revised

## Debate

Page 31, paragraph 2

"If debate were allowed to include personal attacks, it might intimidate many from taking part in the debate (that) might otherwise make important points. It would certainly leave hard feelings and foster personal (hostility) in the group long after the debate had ended and the group's decision had been made."

## Main Motion

Page 126b, Main Motion

"A main motion is a motion whose introduction brings business before (your council)."

## Appendix A7

## On the Road to the Great Depression

I have included many areas for further study, so pick your battles (one at a time) and get to work.

I start by pointing out a lifestyle known as Victorianism, also known as the Industrial Era during the late nineteenth century. In this time frame, people were expected to do the following:

- put duty, honor, family, and community ahead of themselves
- be frugal
- be orderly
- be decent
- be mannerly
- be considerate of others

However, not everyone in history, even today, wants to live up to these high standards of sternly doing their duty and behaving decorously. And you don't have to be a show-off to be dignified.

Point 1 is the most difficult virtue to deal with. Let me explain. Are the wealthy folks pushing duty, honor, and so on aside because these virtues are beneath them? The wealthy want us common souls to abide by all six of these man-made laws. How come these virtues are only for the *common souls*? Maybe the wealthy are loyal and only share among their own community made up of other wealthy people. That's nice. All the rest of us share among our own community, too. Many of the enormously wealthy people, a tiny number compared to the rest of us, possess such a high level of greed that they feel it isn't necessary to follow duty, frugality, order, decency, manners, and the act of being considerate to the not-so-wealthy "beasts" of burden. How about the wealthy at least attempting to be considerate of others? I could go around and around on this subject, but let's continue.

## The US government survived successes and failures

In the late eighteenth century, our unique government began. The constitutional framers and patriots, after a bloody war and much debate, plus the publishing of articles such as the "Federalist Papers," finally agreed to sign the Declaration of Independence, the US Constitution, the amendments, and the Bill of Rights. I'm assuming you know all this. The documents were written to safeguard the citizens from oppressors like the king of England. Because of our ancestors' forethoughts and actions, the original thirteen colonies (individual states) were guaranteed to keep their state political powers. The limited powers of the federal government united the thirteen colonies. How bold this new government's unique powers were as its people traded among other long-established countries. Had the thirteen colonies remained separate entities, their powers would have been a great deal less effective. In the next two centuries, the United States of America grew strong in the eyes of the rest of the world. But you know this!

In the nineteenth century, the federal government had little or no control over business practices among states. Nearing the latter part of the century, the trade monopolies were well established and were taking control of the free enterprise system. Citizens chuckled at the many cartoons published in the newspapers. As it turned out, there was nothing to laugh about as far as the laborers were concerned. The titans of industry flaunted their personal greed and demonstrated their disregard for their workers. The laissez-faire principle of government ruled, or didn't rule, whichever way you look at it. Business giants participating in monopolies squashed any of the government's interventions. The turn of the century ushered in the turmoil of who was controlling whom: big business or the government of the people.

Alas, in the wee small hours of the twentieth century, the federal government applied the laissez-faire system of governing again: hands off big business. And wouldn't you know, the owners of industry continued to abuse the people working for them, paving the way for the federal government to grab more and more power and eventually become the big government it is today. This power grab was a couple of decades in the making and led to the establishment of the unions. Where the working class was concerned, there was a growing discord due to the demise of their constitutional liberties. Today, big government is firmly locked into the power grab, taking freedoms away from the voting citizens as well as the powers of each individual state. This is *unconstitutional* and *morally wrong.* Our nation may implode! To make things worse, the government had help from the corporate world and the banking institutions. So much for the laissez-faire government!

During the twentieth century, the feds asserted political muscle over the leaders of industry with legislation such as, just to name a few, the Clean Air Act, the Occupational Safety and Health Administration, and the Environmental Protection

Agency. And then came the twenty-first century, with the lobbyists scrambling to tear down these regulations levied at big business.

## And another thing ...

Today, technology is out of control. The courts as well as city, state, and federal criminal investigators are sifting through endless constitutional (criminal) laws that are inadequate for the times due to this recklessly fast-changing technology. Congress is out of control. President Obama took the "wait and see" approach. The devastation is accelerating and leading the United States toward a dictatorship. With all my might and heart, I sincerely hope this will never happen. Change just for the sake of change isn't beneficial for America.

Every US citizen must understand how his or her actions today can set up unbearable consequence in the future. The future is now!

The following eight pages reveal some of the many steps taken by each presidential administration in facilitating what became big government—and some questions, too.

## Enter the period of rapid development (late 1800s through early 1900s)

Teddy Roosevelt acted on his attention toward implementing more government involvement in business affairs that crossed state lines and intensified the laissez-faire system of government (at least temporally). These are some of the actions he took while in office:

- interstate commerce control in the form of the Sherman Antitrust Act, but the Supreme Court "took the teeth out" of the antitrust laws
- natural workings of the market weighed against conspiracy
- breaking up of the railroad conglomerates because they crossed state lines
- "beef trust" (watch the documentary *Food, Inc.* to find out what this is about)
- telephone and telegraph rates (Hmm, big government is setting these rates?)
- revealing campaign contributors (okay, this one's good)
- Bull Moose Party (Roosevelt was responsible for the temporary split of the Republican Party. Is Trump doing the same thing to the Democratic Party?)
- government "supervision" of all corporations doing *interstate* business. (Wow!)

In his zeal, Teddy Roosevelt did some unconstitutional things, one being the coal mines in 1902. He threatened to take over mining operations—an illegal act of the president of the United States—revealing his "ends justifies the means" attitude. Was he putting himself above the law? Did Obama follow in Roosevelt's footsteps?

In 1912, the State of Wisconsin set up an unemployment program. They were the first to recognize the need to help citizens financially when, by no fault of their own, workers found themselves without an income.

Enter Woodrow Wilson in 1913, a strong, principled man who amended the Constitution. New branches of government were created. Some of his legislation included the following:

1. direct election of US senators by the citizen vote, which had never been done before
2. Owen-Glass Act, regulating banks that held charters from the national government and set up the Federal Reserve System—Is there too much room for corruption?
3. attempted to control inflation by setting basic interest rates and adjusting the money supply (hmm!)
4. set up the Federal Trade Commission (FTC) in 1914 to investigate corporations and businessmen to cease "unfair" business practices—hooray for Wilson!
5. Clayton Antitrust Act, "beefing up" the Sherman Antitrust Act by disallowing "interlocking directorates" that could create virtual monopolies, and keeping CEOs from sitting on the boards of different companies in the same or related industries—check out the Brown Act in California
6. Federal Farm Loan Act of 1916, addressing long-term financing

In addition, women were taking charge of their own lifestyles. The woman's suffrage movement was gaining forward momentum and was influential in the new legislation allowing women the vote. As a result, the Nineteenth Amendment in 1920 gave all women the vote. Also, people began living easier, less restrictive lives, in part through the wonderful domestic inventions. Unfortunately, Wilson plunged our country into war after stating he would not. Bad Wilson!

Warren Harding in 1921 offered normalcy and a good time following World War I. His presidency ushered in one scandal after another due in part to his choice of office holders: old political cronies who took bribes in exchange for government favors and money. During his term of office, the stronger central government appeared to be the culprit. What I want to know is why men of sound mind gravitate toward greedy, scandalous activities. Didn't their parents teach them the treasured family lessons? If not, do they hold *any* awareness of how their actions affect other citizens, and if so, do they not care? This appears to be an ongoing problem. On the surface, there don't appear to be any answers. Unless US citizens, the family, get together, go unplugged, and talk with one another while studying the US government, liberties will be lost forever.

Back to history.

Enter Calvin Coolidge. He pretty much maintained the same system of government throughout his term of office. The twenty-plus-year span from 1900 through the 1920s provoked the pending arrival of the big government takeover. The legislators wanted to help the citizens, but their efforts were unenforceable due to the hold of the laissez-faire system of governing along with the Supreme Court decisions. Round and round, we go! (There are those judges mucking up the waters again. Or maybe the FBI had more than they could stand and took the law into their own hands.)

Citizen B:    "What a turbulent decade, the twenties."
Citizen A:    "But we were having fun!"
Citizen C:    "Not those who avoided alcohol. Bah humbug!"
Citizen B:    "Don't you like to have fun?"
Citizen C:    "Describe fun for me."
Citizen A:    "Not everyone was having fun. Ness and his G-Men sure struggled."
Citizen B:    'Well, things changed dramatically during the Great Depression era."

## 1920s: A decade of prosperity—or was it?

Life's struggles were beginning to lighten up somewhat because of improvements in several areas.

- electricity, which made domestic chores more palatable (eased people's labor)
- radio, which made domestic chores pleasant (eased people's tedium as they worked)

- automobile, which started many related industries and prompted the federal government to establish state and local income taxes for various purposes:
    - pave dirt roads
    - build new parks
    - scatter gas stations all over the countryside
    - dot the landscape with billboards
    - put up hot dog stands along the highways
    - build tourist cabins

Americans were on the move! Yeeha! Gather up the kids, Ma. We're head'n for Cal-e-for-ni-a.

## Moving forward: A decade of trouble

Oh, dear, now jobs were becoming threatened due to modern technology. And then came the domino effect.

1. Growing unemployment beget a diminished income tax base.
2. Heating oil took over the coal mining market.
3. The cotton industry was threatened when synthetic fibers were developed, *and* less fabric was needed for the new styles of clothing—a double whammy.
4. Farm owners became tenants due to the overproduction of wheat, causing the farmers' price index to decline dramatically.
5. The Black Americans were terrorized with the threat of hanging if they tried to vote.
6. For a while, communism was a strong threat to American ideals.
7. Alien people were jailed or deported because of unpopular opinions.
8. In 1925, Charles Darwin's books were banned from classrooms.
9. In 1900, there was a huge influx of immigrants; US citizens were distrusting of them at first. The American Indians were trusting the white folk who migrated.
10. Immigrant quotas of 1924 favored north Europeans and therefore severely limited Italians, Poles, and Asian people.
11. Prohibition is the nation's glaring failure to control private behavior.
12. The bull market was out of control.

Prior to the stock market crash in 1929, American businesses showed no signs of slowing down, but when the crash happened, everything came to a screeching halt.

1. The popular thought at the time was that stock values would continue to climb.
2. Buying stock on margin and putting up as little as 10 percent turned out badly for the US economy, and yet today the powers that be are offering extremely low down payments for housing. Will we never learn from our history?
3. Furthermore, the price of shares could not reflect their real value. Uh-oh!
4. The economy was weakening at an alarming rate. (Was anyone guarding the stores' cash registers?)

The banks closed for a few days, attempting to hide from the depositors and keep them from making a run on the bank. As it turned out, the banks did not have cash in the vaults because they had squandered the depositors' savings on the stock market, which had just crashed! The United States of America was suddenly stalled in the depths of a severe depression—the worst ever in the history of the world. This depression was worldwide. Our ship was dead in the water.

Why the decade of decline?

1. Industries engaged in overproduction of food, cotton goods, and so on.
2. Foreign markets imposed high tariffs.
3. There was poor management in the agriculture, coal, and textile industries.
4. A dramatic decline in new house construction caused an extremely weakened demand for household goods (especially large ticket items such as refrigerators).
5. A decline in American wages followed as there were no jobs.
6. Modern machines allowed workers to produce many more goods, creating a glut on the market.
7. By late 1929, the few remaining workers could not buy the products they were making (a pathetic turn of events).
8. Tax collections dropped due to unemployment, and unemployment insurance did not exist.
9. Small businesses owners and shopkeepers would see their businesses collapse.
10. College was unreachable to all but the very wealthy.
11. Then, there was the drought, creating the massive Dust Bowl. Farmers didn't know anything about crop-rotation methods. Hope was lost for many years, and that's too long to go without an income. Pockets full of dust anyone?
12. One positive thing held true for the teachers—they kept their jobs. However, they took deep pay cuts. Also, student enrollment was down because parents had to utilize the children's farming skills, leaving little to no time for study.

This decade was a mixed bag of troubles that all but erased a decent and happy lifestyle. But the children of the Depression, through their growing years, learned and appreciated the treasured family social skills, making them worthy citizens who could overcome the insurmountable odds against them.

The stock market crash leading up to the Great Depression did not happen suddenly. Some of the first signs were seen in 1926. The entire country was severely troubled economically. Sound familiar today?

Here are a few questions to ponder:

- Why didn't everyone, from the president of the United States all the way to the individual citizen, realize that compassionate actions would see us through the bad times? President Theodore Roosevelt tried. President Wilson tried. President Hoover endeavored to stem the tide, and President Franklin D. Roosevelt did too. Nothing worked until the very day World War II started.
- Why were the folks selling the worthless stocks on margin?
- How long did the stock market remain closed after the crash?
- Why did the banks foreclose on farm owners? The bankers generally were not in the business of farming. After all, everyone was in the same leaky boat. So why didn't the bank managers paddle alongside the unemployed homeowners? Some of us could have plugged up the holes while others navigated the turbulent rivers. By adapting ourselves to the task at hand and working as a team, we would have taken a much smoother ride while gaining solvency in a much shorter time.
- The owners of industry reduced their workers' pay and even laid off thousands of laborers. Why? In order to hoard their profits? I guess they didn't share the same leaky boat with the rest of the citizens. They were too busy sending their children to Harvard or Yale.
- Why did the banks purchase stocks? Their job was making loans to businesses and homeowners, not contemplating the volatile stock market.
- Why were pension plans used to purchase stock? *Greed?*
- Why did the insurance companies purchase stock? *Greed, again?*
- Who decided to hire photographers to take pictures of the suffering people during the Great Depression? And where did the money come from to pay the photographers for *their* time and equipment?

- If unemployment was so high and the income tax so low, where did the federal money come from to pay the following?
  - the president
  - the congressmen
  - the rapidly growing government agencies and the accountants who were inspecting the banks' books
  - the teachers and other government employees

Wow! We were in a peck of trouble!

It is un–American for the federal government to take powers from the individual states and place them into the hands of the president, the US Congress, or the Supreme Court. To safeguard from this, our founders created the Constitution of the United States of America, the Bill of Rights, and a check-and-balance system.

So where did we go wrong? By reading the world's history, we can clearly see that all societies with such excessive powers at the top will crash and burn. Hold onto your life savings!

In 1929, Herbert Hoover became president. His term of office started months before the crash. Educated in the engineering profession, Hoover was known for his success in managing food organizations during the Great War. These are some of his attempts to revive the country:

- exhorted business owners not to cut wages or lay people off
- asked business owners to take little or no profit
- pleaded with the unions not to demand pay increases
- got Congress to set up the Reconstruction Finance Corporation to offer emergency loans for people and institutions more likely to pay them back, such as
  - banks
  - railroads
  - other groups (hmm, wonder who those other people were?)
- believed government should not play a large role in the economy, favoring instead the laissez-faire system of government; however, the greedy corporations and banks "thumbed their noses" at President Hoover and continued hoarding their profits.

- believed the corporations, unions, and the general working class needed to voluntarily do what was necessary and right to revive our nation. Unfortunately, the laborers had nothing to give for the cause. Instead, greed from owners of industry reduced the laborers' pay, lowering the income tax base and plunging the country into more and more debt.
- Advocated the "trickle down" economic theory; in spite of his efforts, and because of the greed that had infected the economy powerhouses, the trickle nearly evaporated before the money made its way to the general population.

Hoover was unsuccessful due to his refusal to compromise with the banks, monopolies, and the farming and coal-mining industries. Everyone was unwilling to cooperate or, heaven forbid, compromise. It must be lonely at the top when no one will trust your efforts.

History writers C. Collier and J. L. Collier tell us there was a paradox in our nation in the early part of the twentieth century: "Millions of people were going hungry while farmers were suffering from a glut of food" (*Progressivism, the Great Depression, and the New Deal: 1901–1941*). What a pathetic oxymoron!

In many sessions of Congress, senators and representatives express their supposedly heartfelt plans to do good for our country. As it turns out, what the lawmakers are compelling the citizens to accept is not what we the people want. It is a tangled mess. It is *secretive,* which you know is the opposite of transparency. Come on, Americans; these confounded pieces of legislation that our government is passing on to us are not working here in the United States. The US Core Citizens, the family, need to let big government know we are not going to take the misinterpretation of power anymore. I think it's high time the voting public gets a crack at running this country. What say you?

Enter Franklin Delano Roosevelt, a Democrat, in 1933. During his administration, Congress was represented by the Democratic majority. This resulted in a sweeping amount of new legislation and a real, hefty charge toward big government. The following are some of the measures FDR and his advisors came up with.

- They declared a four-day nationwide bank holiday. Spending nearly ground to a halt because most people had no cash, and credit cards hadn't been invented yet. People had little or no money in their pockets to purchase items such as apples, pencils, or even trolley car tokens. Most citizens had to make a choice: do I ride the trolley to the market or buy an apple?

- Government accountants inspected the banks' books, and those found to be honest were reopened.
- The Glass–Steagall Banking Act set up controls against using savings deposits to invest in the stock market—too little too late.
- Under the Federal Deposit Insurance Corporation (FDIC) at the time, each depositor was insured up to five thousand dollars; later in the twentieth century, the amount was raised to one hundred thousand dollars. My, how inflation has compounded!
- The Civilian Conservation Corporation (CCC) employed young men to build new parks, plant trees along the newly paved roads, and do other work.
- The Civil Works Administration gave money to states and municipalities for public construction projects, mostly on the eastern side of the country. Where did *this* money come from?
- Hoover's program that offered farmers inexpensive loans to save their farms from foreclosure, the Farm Credit Act, was expanded. It aided farmers with their mortgages. Again, where did the money come from? The tax base had been cut off at the knees—or maybe the chin.
- The federal government paid farmers to allow portions of their land to lie dormant, endeavoring to encourage the decline of the food glut.
- FDR and his advisors passed the National Industrial Recovery Act (NIRA). This one I am totally confused about. It was passed in an effort to control free enterprise? Would this violate the Sherman Antitrust Act? Later, parts of the NIRA were declared unconstitutional, thank goodness, mainly because Congress cannot give away its powers to the president. I wonder how far-reaching this betrayal has grown.
- The Tennessee Valley Authority built approximately twenty-eight dams and two steam plants, improving life in general for rural people living in the area. This gave the federal government a yardstick with which to hold private electrical companies accountable. How come the feds were not being held accountable?
- The Homeowners Refinancing Act helped some people keep their homes.

Wait a minute, there's no mention of help going toward the West—you know, the states dipping their toes in the Pacific Ocean. What are we, chopped liver?

## Where did all this money come from?

- A handful of wealthy people who were lucky or wise enough managed to come through the crash unscathed. What does luck have to do with anything? Who were these wise ones?
- Government bonds were sold mainly to these lucky people.
- Congress authorized printing extra money by reducing the amount of gold and silver backing the paper dollar. This isn't good!
- I heard that several farming families predicted the crash and hid their money in their backyards. Maybe these were the wise people! Remember, in the early years of the twentieth century, the number of mom-and-pop farms was greater than what it is today.

Monetarism is an economic theory. The money supply of a country is increased in hopes that it will trigger a speed-up in the gross national product (GNP). On the other hand, a reduction causes a slowdown. But this did not work during the time of the Great Depression, nor is it working now. Who's in charge? Better yet, is anybody keeping tabs?

In about 1935, Roosevelt picked up the pace.

- The citizens who were fortunate enough to find work had slim to no chance of saving money for their old age. If they could save a couple of quarters, a rainy day came along too soon and took it all, leaving them no choice but to continue their hard, physical labors. In some cases, when the laborer was no longer able to work, the poorhouses and poor farms were his only alternative for survival. Thus, families' struggles were all too often insoluble. Yes, poorhouses did exist.
- Enter Social Security; it was funded by both employers and employees, each paying equal amounts to give workers "a legal, moral, and political right to collect their pensions and unemployment benefits." In the beginning, agricultural workers, hotel and restaurant employees, plus a few other groups were exempt. In 1958, my first job was in a restaurant as a waitress. FICA had been established by then, but the amount to be withheld from my paycheck for Social Security was nonexistent. You see, I was paid eighty-seven cents an hour. Building my nest egg didn't really start until I left the food industry. And justice for all? This one's personal.

- The National Labor Relations Act (Wagner Act) in part allows unions to strike and requires employers to bargain with union leaders. This act was declared constitutional by the Supreme Court.

- The Public Works Administration (PWA) put laborers and artists to work building roads, post offices, and schools; painting murals; and so on. By then, small numbers of people were working, giving some relief to the hungry; however, the Great Depression raged on. The next time you enter an old post office building, look for murals painted by 1930s artists. Very often they tell a story. (Please don't let anyone tear down these buildings just to put up a high-rise building. Historical buildings are worth preserving.)

- Roosevelt decided to increase the size of the Supreme Court to fifteen justices. Was he attempting to buy the Supreme Court? Congress halted this; the citizens dodged that bullet.

- The greedy owners of industry kept hoarding their wealth, propelling the Depression onward. Why? New laws could not solve the fundamental problems inherent with large industries such as coal mines and tobacco plantations, nor could more laws correct the unhealthy and uneven distribution of the nation's wealth.

- World War II began, and that meant *no more Depression*. But big government continued.

## Briefly jumping ahead to the twenty-first century

The US federal government's welfare program never seems to go away. Too many people have become pathetically dependent on the federal government for every kind of handout. This mass dependency first began in our country during the Depression, the 1930s. Most of the citizens today will not admit how much the government has taken over their daily lives. Dependence on government feels morally wrong to me.

May I suggest engaging in just one or two of these attempts to stem the tide of economic bedlam listed above and compare them to today's economy? You might find them all too familiar.

Appendix A8

Glossary with Comments

(Of the materials gathered in this section, many of the entries come from the dictionary, and others I will quote as individual sources, but most will be my own interpretation of the facts.)

**Competition:** A condition in which (1) companies are seeking the sale of their products at the same time, vying with other companies for the *same* dollar; (2) a trained citizen is seeking a job, struggling against other citizens for that *same* job.

**Federal excessive power grab:** The federal government steps in to curtail monopolies. Alas, the federal government paved the way for future excessive control by taking the powers from the individual states as well as every US voting citizen. And we owe this to a few people and entities: free enterprise greedy owners; the bank executives and their counterparts, the greedy politicians; gluttonous lawyers; out-of-control athletes and entertainers; and don't forget Wall Street and a couple of corrupt Supreme Court justices. To round out this power grab, it is pathetic when the American voters and the nonvoting citizens turn their backs on their responsibility to help govern our country and keep it from imploding.

**Free enterprise:** A carefully thought-out (and hopefully legal) economic system to be tried. Ever since the mid-nineteenth century, inventions have fueled the US free enterprise system. Countless patents and trademarks have been registered, and some became profitable while many others did not. This mostly depended on each entrepreneur's tenacity to successfully market the product or service. One element of good business is to cut the cost of doing business and still maintain an excellent product or service. Many business operators grapple with this concept. With larger businesses came more problems. For one, competition was and still is ruthless. The greedy titans of industry quickly got themselves organized in the form of monopolies in order to control the cost of goods sold. Wall Street, along with the government, kept the pace. Let's toss the high-powered attorneys into this mix, and politicians accepting abundant cash rewards from the corporate upper echelon to write legislation for the different industries. At the same time, hardship for the laborers escalated. In the late nineteenth and early twentieth centuries, the bosses either didn't know or didn't care about how bad working conditions got. Away from the factories, the Victorian industrial corporate leaders lived excessive lives. These opposing lifestyles continued to be at odds throughout this period. To add to the downside, the required working hours were brutal. No improvements were offered to ease the workers' toil. How ironic—the impoverished workers were making products to ease the tedium of homemakers, but at the same time their working conditions were putting them, the employees, in harm's way. Exploiting labor advanced the wealth of the few owners of industry. Suppressed, job holders were in constant fear of losing their meager paychecks if they messed up. By the 1920s, the scales between owner and laborer had become utterly out of kilter.

**Greed:** Wanting to eat or drink a great deal in a hurry; *wanting to get more than one's share.* Who's got greed? Everyone! There are many kinds of greed: recognition, money, power, fame, hoarding of stuff, applause from an audience, and so on. Countless levels of greed and wants crisscross through our daily lives. Of the following, what level of greed do you ascribe to?

- Greed I: your acceptance from others when recognized for a job well done; makes you want to do it again.
- Greed II: the excitement when a writer gets her first book published; she has thoughts of writing more books.
- Greed III: another thrilling level of greed is when a teacher's efforts finally makes sense and the student gets it. I've experienced this one several times.
- Greed IV: hoarding (sometimes ill-gotten) money. And guess who is leading the pack—Washington policy makers!
- Greed V: manifests itself in two opposite ways as an employee, while climbing the corporate ladder, demonstrates his or her desire to get ahead in the company: (1) working hard and staying loyal within the corporation, or (2) remaining loyal only to him- or herself by exercising dishonesty. An example of dishonesty is claiming another employees' work to be his or her own. Boo!
- Greed VI: the farmer demonstrates his greed by acquiring more land to grow greater quantities of wheat, causing a glut on the market and destroying the top soil at the same time. Oh, no!

- Greed VII: destructive greed comes in the form of industry leaders' organizing for the sole purpose of beefing up their wallets by creating a monopoly. A by-product of this is ignoring poor working conditions for people they employ. This is *supposed* to be illegal. However, today the policing of monopolies proves to be tenuous. Why has the Supreme Court decreed a corporation to be a person? Grrr!
- Greed VIII: I believe the worst greed of all is evident in a single person controlling an entire country.

The different degrees of greed range from a harmless, *moderate* collection of shoes (be honest—how many do you own?) to the excessive greed of having complete power over the population of an entire nation. Hoarding is excessive greed. Laughing at the expense of others runs the gamut from having harmless fun to going into hysterics after watching someone lose his or her balance and suffer harm.

A new trend is "greed equals spending." Greed takes the form of wasteful spending on credit cards and frivolous loans. The lure of luxury is the driving force for this irresponsible spending, and the federal government is leading the pack. At which level of greed would you like the US government to operate? Enough greed for now.

**Inalienable:** Cannot be given or taken away or transferred to another; "inalienable rights." *Unalienable* is interchangeable with *inalienable*; both words appear in our eighteenth-century documents.

**Income:** Money or anything that can be measured in currency that you receive when you make a profit from exchanging anything of value, such as skills as a gas-station attendant, tool-and-die man, hairdresser, drafts person, cashier, salesperson, and so on.

**Industrial Revolution:** A time of new businesses, trade, and ground-breaking industry. The late nineteenth and early twentieth century was a time of rapid growth for innovative ideas coming to fruition. Domestic chores became less tedious with the invention of the sewing machine, indoor plumbing, electricity, and so on. Inventors brought forth automation and outfitted manufacturing companies with machines to take the place of many laborers in cotton and steel mills. Today, the troubling industry is telecommunication devices. Not only can the consumer not keep up, but the laws are hopelessly behind. And the employee layoffs—holy Batman! Here's another thought: watch out health-care employees. When the baby boomers start dying off, there may be high unemployment for you too.

**Justice:** A just treatment could be a *deserved* reward or punishment; an exercise of power and authority to maintain what is just and right. To do oneself justice is to carry on as well as one can in our socially conscious government.

**Liberty:** Another word for this is *freedom*. But liberty can mean different things to different people. For example, to a sailor this means she or he has permission to be absent from duty (forty-eight-hour liberty); to your pet, you give the liberty to play in the backyard; citizens have the liberty to use their right to make their own choices and the freedom to speak in public.

**Monopoly:** An entity or group of entities that has exclusive control of a commodity or service. There are so many wrongs with monopolies; the cons outweigh the pros tenfold. The creators of monopolies are greedy people wanting more than they can possibly hold or spend. This inequality continued to be unchecked by the laissez-faire system of federal government until the progressive party came back into power. Could the Constitution have provided safeguards against monopolies? What is surprising is that the Supreme Court basically turned its back on the Constitution, often ruling in favor of the organized corporations. And all this was done in the name of free enterprise? More like unadulterated greed! I smell a rat!

**Need:** First there are eight basic needs: air, water, food, clothing, shelter, love, recognition, and protection from harm. And then there are the elusive ninth and tenth basic needs: want and hope. Thank goodness, we live in a country where we can develop our brains to a higher plane and spring forward the courage to hope. This is a far cry from the subsistence of basic needs. However, we get into trouble if we unduly pursue the *want* category. There could be trouble a-brewing in paradise.

**Pass muster:** To measure up to the required standards (The Free Dictionary by Farlex)

**PDQ:** "Pretty darned quick," as in "If you want to go to the movies, clean up your room PDQ!" According to the website *The Phrase Finder*, "the term was first used in *The Mighty Dollar*, a play by Benjamin E. Woolf; performed in 1875 at the New York's Park Theatre. The play's money-hungry character Judge Bardwell Stote habitually used abbreviations like G.I.C.—'goose is cooked.'" So if you thought texting was original, think again! It had already been thought of.

**Referendum:** The process of submitting a proposition to the voters for approval or rejection. A person knowledgeable in the law writes up the document. Many concerned citizens collect signatures from equally concerned registered voters, and then the first group of citizens submits this list to the city for verification. If enough valid signatures are counted, the referendum gets put on the voting ballot in the form of a proposition. I say "valid signatures" because citizens who want to kill the referendum may sign names like Donald Duck, Huckleberry Finn, and even John Hancock. These citizens may think they are clever, but they are only showing their dishonesty and ignorance.

**Soft power:** A way of telling the government we are not interested in their inability to listen to what the voters need. All of this is done through peaceful means.

**Truth:** I'm wrestling with this word because the truth to me could mean something altogether different to you. For now, I'll let you define this one for yourself.

**Union:** A group of workers joined together to protect and promote laborers' interest. Many of the US factory workers—coal miners being one of the first—united to force the industry leaders to be compassionate about the working conditions of the laborers and to pay them a fair wage. Other unions were being organized in the form of the Communist Union Party before, during, and just after the Great War (late 1910s). However, this movement did not last very long, mainly because communism is contrary to the ideals of the United States of America, which has a free market. Enter the noncommunist unions with their bullying tactics. Industry leaders and unions clashed often and caused many bloody conflicts. The laborer was caught between a rock and a hard place. Law keepers used guns, while laborers fought back with rocks and baseball bats.

**Want:** There is a plethora of wants, too many to account for here. Use your imagination. Wants are above and beyond our basic needs, such as thirteen hundred television channels. Do we really need that many TV channels? And then there is the idea of free enterprise as vanguards dictating what your quality of life should be. "I want what she is having!" The amount of money or possessions we collect do not define our quality of life. The unhealthy quest to make more stuff and sell more stuff is debilitating our precious commodities such as rain forests. We've become a society of planned obsolescence. Before planned obsolescence, things like cars and clothing were built to last. If we got a rip in the seam or the brakes started to squeak, we fixed the problem and kept going. Our treasured family lessons taught us how to fix things. Making excess stuff created stale air and polluted drinking water. So much for quality of life. Unfortunately, we are way past the turning point for excessive greed.

**Rule sixteen:** Live in harmony with-in the family and the greater society and be free from oppression.

**Rule seventeen:** Good grief, Americans! Open your eyes and hearts before there are no more freedoms left in the 21 Century!

# Appendix A9

## A very short list of resources and a few partial quotes

- *The Federalist Papers*, edited by Roy P. Fairfield: An excellent study. Give yourself time to make sense of the message!
- *In Our Defense: The Bill of Rights in Action*, by Ellen Alderman and Caroline Kennedy. An excellent read!
- A quote from the introduction to *Our Country's Founders*, by William J. Bennett. "This, in large part, is a book of advice for how to be a good citizen (young and old) and a trustworthy member of a Socially Independent Government."
- *The Standard Work,* Vol. X (out of print), p. 133. Quote from Justice Sandra Day O'Conner: "Nothing is politically right that is morally wrong.... Every lawbreaker is a traitor to his government and a burden to his fellows."
- *A People's History of the United States*, latest edition by Howard Zinn. A must read that is also on DVD!
- The term "*(political) council* can be traced to England. At first, it referred to a small room where the king met with his closest advisers; later it came to mean the advisers themselves." Quote from *The Dictionary of the U.S. Constitution*, by Barbara Silberdick Feinberg, p. 17.
- "When night approaches, it does not come all at once: neither does oppression. In both instances, there is twilight where everything remains seemingly unchanged." Quote from Justice William O. Douglas as cited in *The End of America*, by Naomi Wolf, p. 2.
- This quote is speaking of devoutly Christian champions of church-state separation. "Their words serve as a continuing reminder of the danger any hint of collusion between church and state poses to the attainment and maintenance of full 'Christian' Liberty." Quote from *The Separations of Church and State*, edited by Forrest Church, pp. xiii–xiv. I recommend reading (with a dictionary handy) President Washington's farewell address on pages 116–120.
- *The Unsettling of America*, by Wendell Berry. Also view Moyers and Company on PBS television interviewing Wendell Berry.
- "Listening: we have two ears and one mouth. Listen twice as much as you speak. Be a good listener. Your ears will never get you into trouble. When I ask you to listen to me and you start giving advice, you haven't done what I asked.

When I ask you to listen to me and you begin to tell me why I shouldn't feel that way, you trample on my feelings." Taken from the March 10, 2010, edition of *The Spotlight*, edited by Carole and Walter Gobitas, p. 4.

- "Becoming morally virtuous is almost wholly within the power of each person. Individuals succeed or fail according to the free choices they make.... Government's doing for the people what the people cannot do for themselves, whether individually or collectively." Quotes from *We Hold These Truths*, by Mortimer J. Adler, pp. 120 and 121. Adler is one of my idols.

- *Robert's Rules of Order, Newly Revised, In Brief,* by H. Robert III, W. Evans, D. Honemann, and T. Balch. My copy is dated 2004.

- "Will term limits result in good politicians being thrown out of office too early, the proverbial baby with the bathwater? Absolutely—but that's a small price to pay for the freedom this will grant us." *Common Sense*, by Glenn Beck, p. 56.

- *Narrative of the Life of Frederick Douglass*, Dover Publications, Inc., 1995.

- *The Corporation*, a documentary written by Joel Bakan and directed by M. Achbar and J. Abbott about conspiracies perpetrated against the citizens by the partnership of big government and big corporations. Everyone needs to become aware of the atrocities done to the peoples of the entire world in the name of economics (greed).

- *The Ecology of Commerce,* by Paul Hawkins, another one of my idols. This work reveals the heart of the corrupt corporations.

- "Our Neighborhood's First Air Raid," *Reminisce*, Reiman Productions, Jan/Feb 1997, p. 18; the article is about Yankee ingenuity, a vital element missing in today's youth. I recommend reading the magazine with senior members of your family who may have lived similar stories.

- *Judge Judy* is a start for understanding some of the duties a judge carries out in court. However, view with moderation. After all, it is a "reality show."

- *The Great Dissent*, by T. Healy. Oliver Wendell Holmes changed the history of free speech in America. Very enlightening!

- *Everybody's Got Something*, by Robin Williams. He will be sorely missed. Thanks for the opportunity to laugh with you, Robin.

- *Christian Science Monitor Weekly*. "Common Ground, Common Good" articles are always good reading. The entire magazine is reliable and factual.

- *Liberty's Kids*, an animated, educational, historical fiction TV series produced by DIC Entertainment with forty episodes that first aired on PBS in 2002. Watch the episode titled "An American Revolutionary War Story" created by Michael

Malianli, Kevin O'Donnell, and Andy Heyard. Some of the voices of the animated characters are provided by Whoopi Goldberg, the late Walter Cronkite, and Reo Janes. The story is told through the eyes of an American teenaged lad, a young English lady, and a French boy, all of whom work as reporters for Ben Franklin. "Benjamin Franklin enlists the help of young people to record the happenings leading up to and during the Revolution for his newspaper the *Pennsylvania Gazette*." Written by Max Vaughn.

- Read more about the problems the food industry is making for US citizens. Go to http://www.takepart.com/foodinc and ask yourself how we, the US citizens, turned a blind eye and got caught up in this mess. The ever-present and growing greed?

- *Zeitgeist Moving Forward*, a 2011 documentary. I suggest taking a few days to watch this film so you can think about its message. Many people may choose not to watch the entire film, as it's rather radical and not *mainstream*.

- Other suggested resources (not limited to the following):
  - A plethora of books on how regular citizens maneuvered through the system
  - Inherited family letters, if you still have them
  - Speeches by public orators like Susan B. Anthony

- Commoncause.org – an excellent group of people here in America working hard on behalf of all US voting (or not) citizens.

Believe it or not, this is a short list! There are so many pieces written about our country that I'm sure you will find plenty to research that is to your liking.

Appendix A10

Sample of letterhead

Stephnie E. Clark, Author                          One XYZ Boulevard
Any City, ZW 99999                                    000-555-1234
Keep Voting, America, ©2018                 Kids&poverty@blogspot.com

January 1, 1999

## Appendix A11

## Quarter-page ad about the possible future of my town

We were everywhere—sitting in front of grocery stores and churches, hanging out in parks, walking the neighborhoods—you name it, we were there, registering citizens for the vote. It's actually fun and socially satisfying to register people to vote! But I can top this. For three months before the election, we—I'm happy to count myself among the seniors in my community—continued our vigilance. Our ranks numbered in the seventies (in age and in numbers of demonstrators, depending on the intensity of the arthritis we were feeling that day). Fortified with power-driven enthusiasm and political signs, we canvassed our busy intersections all around town on the weekends, waving to the passengers in their cars, riding their bikes, and walking along the roadside. Dozens and dozens of people honked their horns and cheered. I would jump for joy when the big truck drivers honked their air horns! We got the attention of the voters, especially the voters still on the proverbial political fence.

For one year, we were the underdogs. Our opponents outspent us by tens of thousands of dollars. The only interview we had at our local public television station was not kind to our plight. Then, wouldn't you know it, right from the start on Election Day the numbers were two to one *in our favor.* We had convinced enough voting citizens in our city to support not just one initiative but *two*! You've got to love the old folks. I have included the quarter page ad we published just before the election. I wrote it on behalf of the mobile-home residents' quest to maintain rent control, our city's way of setting aside a certain amount of low-cost housing. It is a bit long so I won't hold you to reading the whole thing, but I think you'll get a chuckle or two. (I have replaced the name of the city with the letter O and the proposition numbers with X's.)

### It all started with Vacancy Decontrol, aka VD!

This crystal ball interpretation of the future previews the ramifications and consequences of what may transpire. Splintered communities of O are bamboozled into opposing one issue while the city council majority grabs all control of government. Your mission is to decide if this story is fantasy or reality.

On June 5, 2012 O citizens cast their ballots for Prop X & XX. Opponents warned us about City Council Majorities plan to force their pet projects on to their constituency using the tools of the City Charter. Too many voters didn't read printed facts from www ... Instead they voted yes on VD. O's Rent Control evaporated: VD replaced it. And now, the harbor services are on the chopping block. The fall of O has begun.

Time passes, it's 2014. Mr. Councilman completes his 1st year as Mayor. Rents have been raised 'without limits'. The Free Market for housing has collapsed. A few large monopolies are creating the beginnings of a neo-totalitarian government. 'Get used to it, you voted for it!' Or was the special election too much of a hassle to understand the issues preventing you from making the effort to vote!

Time lapses like a fog but sharpens into focus in 2016. The passage of Prop XX gave the council majority the feeling they had the right to carry out their sinister plans. The ordinance also opened the flood gates to privatize and outsource community services. The city council's rule, 5:zip came with a warning. Competitors, outside of O formed monopolies charging space rents so high that people with limited income couldn't pay creating a huge void in the affordable housing market. No more Federal funds. Fortunately, some mobile home residents are successful finding a place to live with their kids or friends but placing a strain on everybody's budgets. More mobile home owners find shelter in cars parked in city alleys and private driveways. Still others have been 'put out to pasture' and have been forgotten. Could this be O's main contributing factor for increasing the homeless population?

January 2018 Mr. Councilman wins 2nd term as Mayor. Council Majority continually holds a death grip on the citizens of O. All planning and decision making comes from The Majority Council, leaving the citizens *out of the process*. Complications regarding litigation with the poorly written digital billboard ordinance negated any financial gains causing fiscal bedlam. Does this courtroom stuff sound familiar? The legal process between the city and Mobile Home Park Owners started this type of suing frenzy in the last century. The *abolished ordinance 00B (rent control) guaranteed the park owners a minimum profit of 14%,* allowing them to keep their *business doors open* and still have enough money to purchase another helicopter. What other business gets a guarantee of any profit?

The year 2020: There was a time when locals and visitors could take a stroll on the beach. Not anymore! All beaches are privately owned. The digital billboard situation escalates. On average, we see 8 traffic collisions daily. Can't pay the outsourced ambulance fees? Too bad! Before the June 2012 election, opponents advised us not to allow the city council free license to ignore the valuable *safe guards* offered by the voters. All this could have been avoided simply by utilizing public commissions!

Another year passes. Mr. Councilman retires. His special projects chased away decent people and honest businesses.

It's 2025. Only a select business community is allowed in and they must follow the reciprocity to the 5:zip council; foretold by the opposition in 2012. Could things get worse? Yes! City council outsourced *all* essential services. Back in 2012 the opponents predicted citizens would be in big trouble. The other day another house burned down because the owners were unable to pay for the fire departments service. *The City is* totally contracted out. Wow! And it only took 13 years to destroy our city. Remember: 'they' said Vacancy Decontrol was good for our town.

Fantasy or Reality, get familiar with the facts: www. … If you want a different future than this, vote 'NO" on X & XX June 5th. It's *your* choice!

~~~~~~~~~~~~~~~~~~~~~~~~~~~~~~~~~~~~~~~~~~~~~~~~~~~~~~~~

After reading this ad, the citizens understood their choices and voted with confidence. The citizens who put this together as an educational tool were not part of a political action committee (PAC) but a nonprofit organization gathering informative facts. We offered these facts willingly to everyone, our members as well as the general population of the town.

As a final note, we are a society that welcomes all people of the world who want to live without oppression from an overbearing political or military ruler. People from all over the globe have come to the United States: Indonesia, Russia, Saudi Arabia, China, India, Australia, South Africa, Panama, Ireland, and so on. Americans number among the disabled, patent holders, poverty stricken, politicians, entrepreneurs, military personnel, manual laborers, probation officers, and especially salespeople. We support many diverse industries, including manufacturing, raw materials, entertainment, medical, farming, hospitality, security, travel, construction, education, ready-made garments, and even psychic services. So let's all play nicely!

I promise, this is the last note, unless you want to have coffee with me and talk about things. One way to empower the voting citizens is by initiating the United States Family Liberty Plan, going unplugged for one hour a week, and talking *with* one another. Keep voting, America.

Printed in the United States
By Bookmasters